# THE
# UPHOLSTERER'S
# POCKET REFERENCE BOOK

**MATERIALS • MEASUREMENTS • CALCULATIONS**

## David James

Guild of Master Craftsman Publications Ltd

First published 1995 by
Guild of Master Craftsman
Publications Ltd,
166 High Street, Lewes,
East Sussex BN7 1XU

Reprinted 1998, 1999

ISBN 0 946819 71 8

Front cover photograph by
Ray Highnam. Chair supplied by
Richard Green.

Designed by Fineline Studios.
Printed and bound in Great Britain by
Redwood Books, Trowbridge, Wiltshire

# THE
# UPHOLSTERER'S
# POCKET REFERENCE BOOK

**MATERIALS • MEASUREMENTS • CALCULATIONS**

# Contents

To all aspiring upholders.

# Preface

Trade and craft pocket books have been produced in a variety of subjects since the late 19th century. Early examples were written for the painter and decorator, the French polisher and the carpenter and joiner; these and others like them occasionally pop up in antiquarian bookshops or can be seen on display in small regional museums. This book has been written as a useful pocket reference for anyone learning or practising upholstery, in the hope that it will help perpetuate a tradition.

I would like to express my sincere thanks to all those whose help with the pictures, ideas and technical information have made this book possible. Also the following: Singer (UK) Ltd, BFM, Vitafoam Ltd, Connolly Brothers (Curriers) Ltd, Parkertex Fabrics Ltd, Chiltern Springs, Pullmaflex (UK) Ltd, Isaac Lord Tools Ltd, the High Wycombe branch of John Lewis, and the Buckinghamshire College of Brunel University.

A special thanks to Eirlys and to my editors Alex Woolf and Elizabeth Inman.

## Publisher's Note

Tables and formulae for converting measurements from imperial to metric, and vice versa, are to be found on pages 151–155.

# Introduction: History of Furniture

## Principal British Styles

|  | Approximate dates | Monarchs |
|---|---|---|
| Elizabethan | 1588 – 1603 | Elizabeth I |
| Jacobean | 1603 – 1625 | James I |
| Carolean | 1625 – 1649 | Charles I |
| Cromwellian | 1649 – 1660 | Commonwealth |
| Restoration | 1660 – 1689 | Charles II (d.1685) James II (d.1689) |
| William and Mary | 1689 – 1702 | William and Mary (Mary d.1694) |
| Queen Anne | 1702 – 1714 | Anne |
| Early Georgian | 1714 – 1727 | George I |
| Georgian | 1727 – 1760 | George II |
| Late Georgian | 1760 – 1810 | George III (d.1820) |
| Regency | 1810 – 1830 | George IV |
| William IV | 1830 – 1837 | William IV |
| Victorian | 1837 – 1901 | Victoria |
| Edwardian | 1901 – 1910 | Edward VII |

## Principal French Styles

|  | Approximate dates |
|---|---|
| Louis XIV | 1660 – 1700 |
| *Régence* | 1700 – 1715 |
| Louis XV | 1715 – 1765 |
| Transitional | 1765 – 1775 |
| Louis XVI | 1775 – 1790 |
| *Directoire* | 1790 – 1800 |
| *Consulat* and Empire | 1800 – 1815 |
| Restoration | 1815 – 1830 |
| Louis Phillipe | 1830 – 1848 |
| Second Empire | 1848 – 1870 |

# Principal European Styles and Influences

**Renaissance** Revival of ancient Greek and Roman styles in 14th- and 15th-century Italy. Widespread by 16th century.

**Baroque** Massive and exuberant forms of classical inspiration during 17th and early 18th centuries.

**Rococo** Light, asymmetrical, scrolling designs developed in France in early 18th century.

**Chinoiserie** Often fanciful interest in China from late 17th to early 19th centuries.

**Gothic Revival** Romantic interpretations of medieval (pre-Renaissance) styles in late 18th- and early 19th-century Britain.

**Neoclassicism** Renewed interest in the styles of classical antiquity from mid-18th to early 19th centuries.

**Regency** Opulent melding of classical and romantic styles in early 19th-century Britain.

**Historical revivals** Several styles were favoured in 19th-century Britain (with equivalents elsewhere): Classical, Gothic, Elizabethan and Louis XIV.

**Arts and Crafts** Emphasis on hand skills and traditional designs in late 19th-century Britain.

**Art Nouveau** Organic flowing forms and geometrical abstraction are two variations on this turn-of-the-century style.

**Art Deco** Fine materials and streamlined forms characterize this early 20th-century style originated in France.

# The History of Upholstery

| Furniture Style and Period | Construction | Fabric Coverings | Examples of Upholstery | |
|---|---|---|---|---|
| Elizabethan (Renaissance) 1588–1603 | oak, beech | silk velvets, tapestry | upholstered oak X-frame chair, c. 1590 | |
| Early Stuart (Jacobean) 1603–1649 | oak, fruit woods | tapestry | the Knole settee, c. 1600 early oak chair, c. 1600–1640 | |
| Commonwealth (Cromwellian) 1649–1660 | oak | silk embroidery, ox hide | nailed upholstery farthingale chair, c. 1650 | |
| Late Stuart (Carolean) 1660–1688 | walnut | turkey work, cane work | French armchair, c. 1660 walnut framed, winged sleeping chair, c. 1675 | |
| William and Mary (Dutch influence) 1689–1702 | walnut | damasks | walnut upholstered armchair, c. 1690 | |
| Queen Anne (Baroque) 1702–1714 | walnut, marquetry | embroidered velvets | Queen Anne side chair, c. 1715 with loose seat upholstery | |
| Georgian: George I 1714–1727 | mahogany | brocade, baize | early wing armchair, Georgian style, c. 1730 | |

| Furniture Style and Period | Construction | Fabric Coverings | Examples of Upholstery |
|---|---|---|---|
| George II 1727–1760 | mahogany | Soho tapestry | walnut and mahogany side chairs C. 1730 |
| George III 1760–1820 | mahogany, painted woods | printed Indian chintz | Hepplewhite settee, mahogany C. 1770 |
| Regency 1811–1820 | satinwood birch | Spanish leather, Berlin woolwork | Danhauser sofa, Vienna, c. 1820 |
| George IV 1820–1830 | painted and gilded hardwoods | hair cloth | Regency couch, c. 1830 bolsters and scrolls |
| William IV 1830–1837 | rosewood, metal | cross stitch, tent stitch | library seat, buttoned in hide, c. 1835 |
| Victorian 1837–1901 | all woods, papier-mâché, iron | Holland linen, calico, velour | walnut ladies' chair, buttoned, c. 1860 chaise longue, French cabriole legs c. 1850 |
| Art Nouveau 1890–1901 | ash, beech, bentwood | leathercloth, wool plush | The Morris chair, adjustable, in oak, c. 1870 |
| Edwardian 1901–1910 | steel, mahogany, beech | chenille, Morocco (goatskin), moquette | Edwardian suite, carpet panels, c. 1900 |

| Furniture Style and Period | Construction | Fabric Coverings | Examples of Upholstery |
|---|---|---|---|
| Art Deco 1918–1939 | plywoods, early plastics | modern tapestry, cut moquette | tub chair, nailed upholstery, c. 1925 tube chair, c. 1932 |
| Modern (George VI, Elizabeth II) 1940–1960 | oak, teak | moquettes, leathercloth | fully sprung armchair, c. 1940 wing chair buttoned in moquette, c. 1955 |
| Pop Art 1960–1970 | Glass, steel, moulded plastics | PVC cloths, tweeds, corduroy | Sacco chair, c. 1960 and all-foam chair |
| Contemporary (Elizabeth II) 1970–1990 | steel, hardwoods, board materials | acrylic velvets, tweeds and prints | modern settee and chair, c. 1980 |
| 1990- | hardwoods, steel, board materials | weaves, natural cloths, leathers prints | contemporary settees, c. 1990 |

# CHAPTER 1

# Workshop, Equipment and Safety

## The Workshop

### Workshop processes

Work in upholstery generally falls into the following categories and a workshop should be arranged to cope with these jobs:

- Stripping.
- Frame repairs or frame making.
- Discarding large amounts of old upholstery.
- Cleaning and carding reusable materials.
- Bench work, springing and upholstery construction.
- Marking out and cutting materials and foams, etc.
- Measuring, marking out and cutting new covers.
- Machine sewing and making up.
- Making up new cushion interiors.
- Button making and cushion filling.
- Finishing, trimming and cleaning.

### Working conditions

Approximately 375 square feet (35 sq m) is the very minimum floor space for one person to work comfortably. If at all possible, long-term storage of materials and work should be arranged in a first-floor room or a partitioned-off area.

Good lighting in the form of large windows and fluorescent lighting is essential, since upholstery work and materials must be inspected continually during the production process. If possible, lighting should come from all sides of the workshop.

Adequate ventilation is also important. Upholstery is dusty work and can be very dirty at times. A workshop should have at least one extractor fan; otherwise several opening windows at various levels will assist air circulation.

### Services to the bench area

For the provision of power for tools at the bench, two different power lines are required: electrical in the form of 13-amp points, and pneumatic for air tools. If

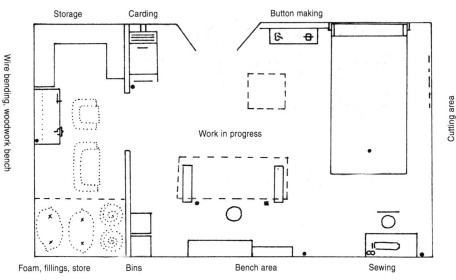

**Fig 1.1 Typical upholstery shop layout.**

possible, these should be suspended overhead, one to the right of the bench and one to the left. Wall-mounted points are a little less safe because of trailing wires and hoses. A hook for each power tool, either overhead or at the wall, will hold them safely and conveniently in place when not in use.

Services to the cutting table are normally only electrical, and for safety reasons should always be overhead – electric cloth-cutters are very sharp and will easily slice through a power cable. Some form of take-up system for the wiring to the cutters is necessary to ensure that lengths of electrical cable do not build up on the cutting area.

# Equipment

## Work bench and bench space

There is no better method of supporting pieces of upholstery than a pair of trestles (Fig 1.2). Construction of trestles should be strong and well braced, so that a work piece of any weight or shape is not only held rigid, but can be rolled over or lowered at any time. Trestles can be made from good-grade softwood or a straight-grained hardwood, e.g. pine or beech. A well should be formed at the top to contain a soft pad, which will offer protection and stop the work from sliding off.

## Bench board

When upholstering small items such as loose seats or headboards, a bench board will complement the trestles and allow the upholsterer to sit at the

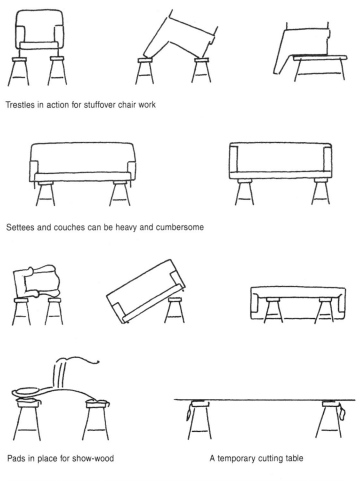

Trestles in action for stuffover chair work

Settees and couches can be heavy and cumbersome

Pads in place for show-wood        A temporary cutting table

**Fig 1.2 Using the trestle bench to its best advantage. The work should be moved to give the best and most comfortable working position.**

bench, as one would sit at a desk. A useful bench board size is 4 x 3ft (1.2 x 0.9m). One side of the board should be padded and covered with a strong durable covering, leaving a plywood or hardboard surface on the other. The padding provides a non-slip surface and will deaden noise, besides being kind to show-wood polished surfaces.

## Bench blocks

These give support to long or delicate chair rails while tacking, and hold shaped work, especially loose seats and chair backs. They should be padded and covered along their top surfaces. A long narrow strip of hardwood, bolted to the surface of a bench board, can be used as a stop against which small pieces of work can be pushed during stripping.

## Table bench

This is an alternative to the trestle-type bench, usually made of wood and similar to a polisher's bench, except that the top is padded to provide a non-slip protective surface. Dimensions are usually about 4 x 3 x 2ft high (1.2 x 0.9 x 0.6m).

## Cutting table

The structure and size of this table will depend on the space available and the type of work being done. The table should be of good weight and have a rigid base or underframe, made from metal or timber. The cutting-table surface must be flat, smooth and absolutely square, so that measuring and straight cutting can be taken from the table edge. The most suitable materials for the table top are plywood, blockboard or chipboard, which should be lipped at the edges and have a cutting surface of hardboard, lino or plastic laminate laid over the whole table.

The table top should be 54–60in (137–152mm) to allow for most widths of cover, and at least 8ft (2.44m) long for small businesses, and up to 70ft (21.3m) long in larger concerns. Thickness of the top should normally be about 1in (25mm).

A shelf can be fitted under the table to store tools and materials. It is important that the height of the table suits the person using the table regularly.

## Gluing foams

If space is available, a small area should be kept aside for the gluing of foams, particularly if the glue is to be applied by spray (*see* pages 39 and 74). A small table with standing room for the pressure pot, and an air-line socket to the power, is all that is needed.

## Button making

To save on space, button-making presses (*see* pages 33 and 141) can be fixed to any firm surface or mounted on a heavy wood base about 2 x 1ft (60 x 30cm) and stored under the cutting table until needed.

# Safety

## Workshop exits or doorways

There should be at least two exits, preferably at opposite ends of the shop, one of which should be a double door or sliding door with a minimum span of 5ft (1.5m).

## Clearways

At least one walkway must be kept clear of all materials and work, to allow easy escape and access.

## Firefighting equipment

The risk of fire can be minimized by careful storage of materials, and having two types of extinguisher available at all times in the workshop. Advice on how to use them is freely available from fire stations.

## Dust and fume extraction

An extractor fan should be fitted close to a carding machine, and where solvents and glues are being used.

## First aid

Although upholstery work does not involve any particularly dangerous processes, any wound, however small, should be dealt with quickly. A box containing basic first-aid equipment should be clearly marked and easily accessible.

## Safety apparatus and protective clothing (Fig 1.3)

Hands should be protected by using stitching gloves, or rubber gloves when glue is being applied in large quantities, while barrier creams are a good alternative for the dirtier jobs. These assist the easy removal of oil, grease, glue or solvents.

A simple elasticated mask with changeable gauze pads will protect the nose and mouth when very dusty work has to be done. Always protect the feet from nails, tacks etc. by wearing good shoes.

The traditional craftsman's apron is also a form of protective clothing. Made from lightweight canvas or strong calico, it provides protection for normal clothing.

## Machines and power tools

As a general rule, moving parts on industrial machines need to be guarded and the guards painted a bright colour to indicate their function. Some of the old carding machines still in use are potentially dangerous and should be checked and modified, particularly if they are to be motorized.

Weekly routine maintenance on all machines and powered equipment is the greatest aid to safety. Regular maintenance should be carried out in logical sequence to ensure nothing is overlooked. The following is a good routine and provides a useful checklist:

1 Remove from power source.
2 Check condition of wiring or hose.
3 Remove detachable parts, e.g. blades or guards.
4 Clean, lubricate and/or sharpen.

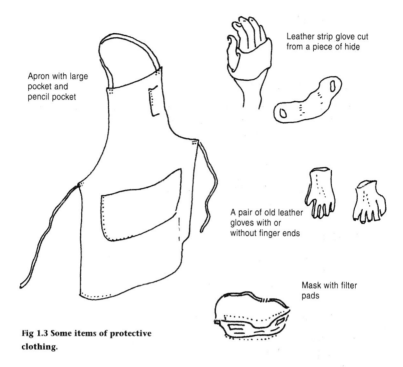

Apron with large
pocket and
pencil pocket

Leather strip glove cut
from a piece of hide

A pair of old leather
gloves with or
without finger ends

Mask with filter
pads

**Fig 1.3 Some items of protective
clothing.**

5  Check levels of lubricants and coolants
6  Reassemble.
7  Reconnect to power, and test

In largescale machine-assisted upholstery production, electric and pneumatic power supplies to machinery must be carefully regulated, with built-in safety mechanisms to ensure that the installations are basically sound. All machines will normally be fused and earthed, and a check should be made regularly on wiring hoses and pipework. Turn-off buttons or switches are fitted to each machine and must be easily accessible and well marked. Similarly, wall-mounted, brightly coloured 'panic buttons', where electrical supply can be stopped quickly, are fitted to all work areas.

Exposed moving parts on any machine should be, as far as possible, guarded or fenced. All potential dangers should be highlighted by labelling, colouring and the use of warning signs on machines and machine parts. Unsafe machinery must be reported as a requirement of the Health and Safety at Work Act, 1980.

## Cleanliness

Washing facilities with hot and cold running water are needed if work is to be kept clean. The work area should be cleaned down and rubbish removed as often as possible.

# Fire safety regulations for upholstery fabrics and upholstered furniture

A free booklet is available from local authority trading standards departments, entitled, *A Guide to the Furniture and Furnishings (Fire) (Safety) Regulations*. This guide should be read by all suppliers, manufacturers, upholsterers, reupholsterers and retailers.

The guide explains the following:

1   The product ranges covered by the regulations.

2   The suppliers affected by the regulations; for example:
● Persons who supply filling materials and fabrics to the furniture industry or direct to consumers.
● Persons who supply furniture, furnishings or reupholstery services.

3   Exemptions; for example:
● Exports of furniture.
● Furniture made before 1950.
● Reupholstery of furniture made before 1950.
● Furniture in secondhand caravans.

4   Action dates (dates on which new regulations come into force).

5   What suppliers need to do; for example:
● Ensure that foam fillings and non-foam fillings pass the appropriate tests.
● Ensure that fabrics supplied to provide or replace permanent covers on furniture pass the appropriate match test.
● Determine whether fabrics supplied are to be used to provide a visible or non-visible part of the upholstery.

6   What the regulations include in their definition of furniture and furnishings; for example:
● All upholstered seating furniture.
● Upholstered articles such as music stools, foot stools, pouffes, bean bags, and floor cushions, which are intended for use in a private dwelling.
● Domestic upholstered furniture (whether complete or ordered with the customer's own choice of cover fabric).
● Visible and non-visible platform cloths and dust covers on the underside of furniture.

7   Parts of the furniture that are not subject to the requirements of the regulations.
● Braids and trimmings.
● Scrims or stockinet for foams and other fillings.
● Springs.

8   The regulations relating to nursery furniture, beds and bedding; for example, loose covers and stretch covers. These are covers that are supplied

separately from the furniture.

Loose covers for upholstered furniture must be match resistant when tested over standard polyurethane foam.

9   The regulations relating to the upholstery of all furniture made after 1 January 1950. All filling material and cover fabric used in reupholstering such furniture must meet the new levels of fire resistance.

However, when only re-covering is requested by the customer, the reupholsterer is not obliged to replace non-conforming filling material which the furniture may contain. It is recommended though, that in such circumstances, the reupholsterer should draw the fire risk to the customer's attention. Any filling which the reupholsterer adds to the existing filling must, of course, meet the new requirements. In ordering upholstery materials the reupholsterer should seek advice from his supplier about their suitability for use in furniture.

10  The regulations applying to secondhand furniture sold in the course of trade, including auction. From 1 March 1993, secondhand furniture made from 1 January 1950 onwards and sold in the course of trade must meet the requirements of the regulations.

11  The regulations applying to labelling. For new and secondhand furniture sold between 1 March 1990 and 28 February 1993, the regulations do not require the following items to carry a display label:.
- Mattresses and bed bases.
- Pillows, scatter cushions and seat pads.
- Loose covers and stretch covers for furniture.

Copies of the guide may be obtained from: The Consumer Safety Unit, Department of Trade & Industry, Room 302, 10-18 Victoria St, London SW1H 0NN. Enquiries about the specific contents of the guide should be made to your local county trading standards department.

# CHAPTER 2

# Tools, Machines, Fixings and Fittings

## Hand Tools

### Hammers (Fig 2.1)

There are three types of tacking hammer available, of which the magnetic hammer with two faces is the most commonly used today. The other two versions are a little lighter and more traditional in their design. A standard tacking hammer has a single face, a claw and a smooth round handle. The cabriole hammer has a fine small face of about ¼in (7mm) diameter, and a long, pear-shaped handle. A small single-face magnetic hammer may

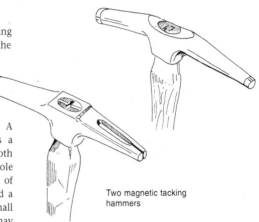

Two magnetic tacking hammers

also be found useful. It is not necessary to have all three designs of hammer, but every craftsman tends to make a collection of tools over a period of time.

Owing to the low weight of tacking hammers which are designed especially for upholstery work, a heavier, medium-sized claw hammer of the kind used by carpenters should be included in the tool kit. This will be needed for frame repairs, wire forming and any heavy work which would put too much strain on a tacking hammer.

**Fig 2.1 Hammers**

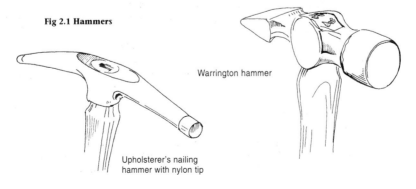

Warrington hammer

Upholsterer's nailing hammer with nylon tip

## Upholstery scissors or shears (Fig 2.2)

These ought to be of the highest quality that can be afforded, as they will be used for cutting and trimming all kinds of material for a large percentage of workshop time. For this reason it is essential they are always in good condition and kept sharp.

For upholstery work, a minimum length of 8in (200mm) for trimming scissors is usual. The traditional design is flat and straight, with a blunt end filed smooth and used for tucking away fabric between chair rails and into corners. The cast-bent shear has proved more popular; its comfortable shape, incorporating a large and small hand grip, and its long blade, make it easier to work with for long periods. Shear lengths range from 8–10in (200–255mm).

A good pair of 8–10in (200–255mm) scissors can be kept for trimming and cutting of materials such as rubberized hair, waddings, thin foam, etc., while a pair of 12in (305mm) cutting shears can be used for cover cutting.

Leather trimming scissors

Pinking shears are useful for the cutting of fine fabrics and for cloth that is likely to fray. The blades are serrated and make a zig-zag cut, leaving the edge reasonably clean and less susceptible to fraying.

Thread snips are used by the sewing machinist. They are lightweight and usually sprung, so that the blades are held open in readiness to trim thread or snip seams when necessary.

**Fig 2.2 Scissors and shears used in upholstery.**

Thread snips

Cast-bent upholstery shears

## Web strainers or stretchers

Web strainers are usually made from beech and are between ⅝in and ¾in (16mm and 20mm) thick, and the dowel peg has a diameter of ⅝in (16mm). Most upholsterers use the standard slot-and-dowel type of strainer, but with a little practice the other simpler types are equally effective.

A pair of metal strainers, often called iron hands, with jaw widths of 2in (50mm) and 1in (25mm), are useful as a general straining or stretching tool (Fig 2.3). As they depend on the strength of the user's hand, they are limited for webbing applications, but are often needed in hide work, for example, or in any situation where a cover requires a heavy pull beyond normal tightness.

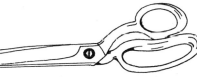

**Fig 2.3 Metal web strainers with 2in (50mm) jaws.**

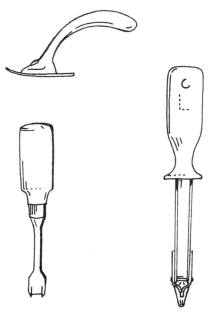

**Fig 2.4 Three different types of staple lifter.**

## Staple lifters (Fig 2.4)

A variety of staple-lifting tools are available, mostly from the staple-manufacturing companies. It is extremely difficult to lift and remove the larger staples from a frame intact. If a staple lifter is used, a small pair of pincers will be needed to lift the bits of staple left in the rails. The staple lifters illustrated in Fig 2.4 all depend on the user's ability to dig the tool into the rail and under the staple crown.

## Ripping chisels (Fig 2.5)

This is designed for the fast, easy removal of tacks and staples. It should be struck with a wooden mallet and not with a tacking hammer. The most effective type of ripper is straight bladed. This is a very strong tool with a heavy blade and a built-in shock absorber set in front of the brass ring where the blade is joined to the handle. The tip of the blade is ground flat to a near-sharp point, which will require grinding after heavy use.

Other types of ripping chisel are the cranked-blade chisel, which usually has a pear-shaped handle and a bevelled tip, and the split-point tack lifter, for removing tacks at a gentler pace.

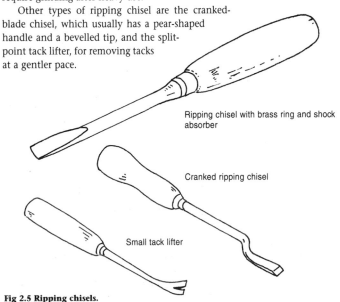

Ripping chisel with brass ring and shock absorber

Cranked ripping chisel

Small tack lifter

**Fig 2.5 Ripping chisels.**

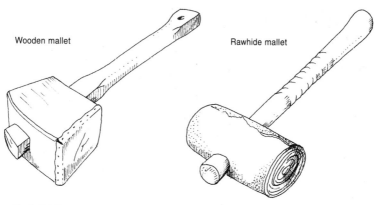

Wooden mallet

Rawhide mallet

**Fig 2.6 Mallets.**

## Mallets (Fig 2.6)

Upholsterer's mallets need to be fairly lightweight and comfortable to handle for long periods. Some craftsmen cover one face of the mallet head with a piece of hide, which will preserve the face and reduce noise.

## Trimming and cutting knives (Fig 2.7)

These are more effective than scissors when trimming hide or vinyl-coated fabrics, especially when a clean, straight cut is required or an edge is to be thinned or skived. A hide-skiving knife has a curved, bevelled edge on a strong, rigid blade. A sharp knife is useful when upholstery is being stripped from an old frame, to save unnecessary strain on scissors.

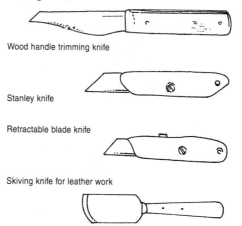

Wood handle trimming knife

Stanley knife

Retractable blade knife

Skiving knife for leather work

**Fig 2.7 Trimming and cutting knives.**

## Upholstery needles (Fig 2.8)

A range of nine upholstery needles of various types and sizes provides the basic stitching and sewing equipment. The use of twine and thread to join and fix upholstery materials and to form stuffed shapes applies mainly to traditional upholstery. In modern production work, such needles will only be needed for buttoning and the occasional small amount of slip stitching.

The 12in (305mm) two-point bayonet needle, 10- or 12-gauge, is designed for edge stitching. The 10in (255mm) by 13-gauge, round-point, double-ended needle is used for small stitched edges and scroll work. The buttoning needle has a single round point and a large eye. It may be necessary to use a bayonet point for buttoning if particularly dense fillings or foams prove difficult.

Curved and circular needles are peculiar to the upholstery trade. These include springing needles, usually 5in (125mm) by 8- or 10-gauge with four-sided bayonet points, used to sew in and fix springs and spring wires; the half-round, two-point needle, normally 12-gauge and 5–6in (125–150mm), used for edge stitching close to a show-wood rail; and the rounded-point circular needle, which comes in three basic sizes. These are the 6in (150mm) 16-gauge used with twine to produce stuffing ties and join hessian and scrims; the 3in (75mm) 18-gauge – the 'slipping circ' – used with slipping thread to close upholstery covers on chair outsides, cushions, etc.; and the 2½in (63mm) 19-gauge – the 'cording circ' – used with a strong thread to sew in cords and trimmings.

**Fig 2.8 Upholstery needles.**

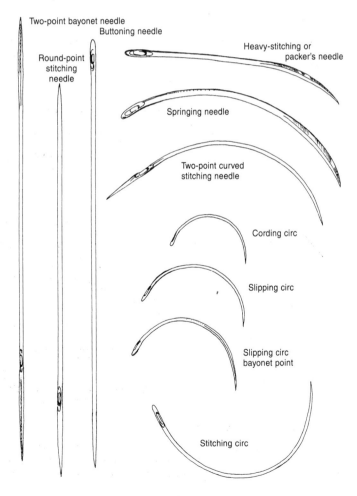

Two-point bayonet needle

Buttoning needle

Round-point stitching needle

Heavy-stitching or packer's needle

Springing needle

Two-point curved stitching needle

Cording circ

Slipping circ

Slipping circ bayonet point

Stitching circ

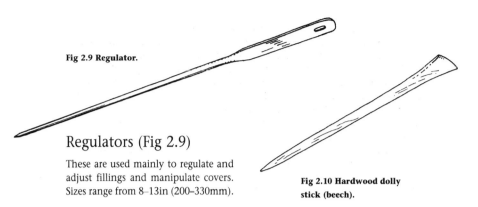

Fig 2.9 Regulator.

## Regulators (Fig 2.9)

These are used mainly to regulate and adjust fillings and manipulate covers. Sizes range from 8–13in (200–330mm).

**Fig 2.10 Hardwood dolly stick (beech).**

## Wooden dolly sticks (Fig 2.10)

These are used to help fold and pleat fabrics and leather (*see* page 135). They have a smooth, round point and a flat, spade-shaped end, and are 7–8in (175–200mm) long.

## Skewers and pins (Fig 2.11)

These are holding tools where temporary fixing of materials is needed prior to sewing or stitching (*see* page 107). Pins are 1¼in (32mm) plated, and skewers are normally 3 or 4in (75 or 100mm).

**Fig 2.11 Skewer (top), and plated pin.**

## Rasps (Fig 2.12)

**Fig 2.12 Rasp.**

A medium-sized rasp with a 10in (255mm) blade is used for removing sharp edges on timber rails prior to upholstery.

## Pincers (Fig 2.13)

These are used for gripping and removing nails, pins and staple ends. They may also be used to cut soft wire and to lever out small nails using the claw at the end of the hand grip.

**Fig 2.13 Pincers.**

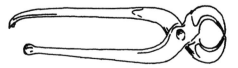

## Tube-shaped hole cutters (Fig 2.14)

These are used to punch or drill polyurethane foams in preparation for buttoning (*see* page 74). The simplest type is a 1–1¼in (25–32mm) steel tube, sharpened to a cutting edge at one end, which can be hand-pushed or hammered into the foam.

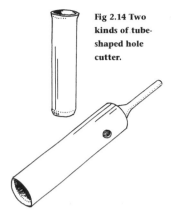

**Fig 2.14 Two kinds of tube-shaped hole cutter.**

Another type can be fitted to a power drill, for situations when a lot of foam-drilling is done regularly.

## Tools for measuring and marking out (Fig 2.15)

A metre stick is marked in metric measurements on one side and imperial on the other. A T-square is used for marking across the width of the cutting table and will give accurate lines at 90° to the table edge. A straightedge up to 6ft (2m) long can be used for marking along the length of the roll or cutting table. A large set square, usually at 60°, provides a check on

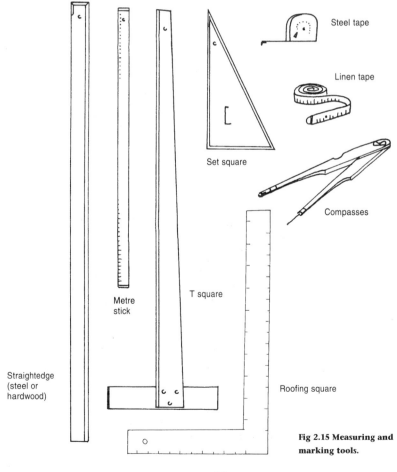

Steel tape

Linen tape

Set square

Compasses

T square

Metre stick

Straightedge (steel or hardwood)

Roofing square

**Fig 2.15 Measuring and marking tools.**

squareness. A large pair of compasses should be included in the range of tools. Two types of flexible measuring tape, one steel and one linen, at least 4ft (1.5m) long, are necessary for taking measurements from chairs etc.

The following is a list of marking tools and their suitable surfaces:

- Tailor's crayon – most fabrics
- White stick chalk – vinyls, hides
- Soft pencil (4B) – hides and linings
- Felt pen – foams
- French dusting chalk – Kraft paper stencils – most fabrics

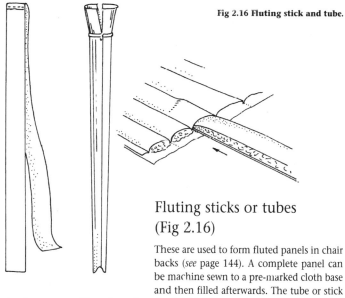

**Fig 2.16 Fluting stick and tube.**

## Fluting sticks or tubes (Fig 2.16)

These are used to form fluted panels in chair backs (*see* page 144). A complete panel can be machine sewn to a pre-marked cloth base and then filled afterwards. The tube or stick is simply a means of inserting a length of thick filling such as cotton felt, curled hair or wadding, into each separate flute. The width of the tool should be approximately ⅜in (10mm) less than the flute or channel to be filled. A one-metre length stick will be long enough to deal with any normal-sized panels.

## Wire cutting and bending (Fig 2.17)

Bolt croppers are the best tool for cutting wire. Their jaws can be adjusted to deal with all wire gauges. A fairly easy method of bending wire is to use a short length of ½in (13mm) steel tube, which is simply slid along the wire to a point where the wire is to be bent, and then by levering with the hands a radius can be formed. A similar tool is the bench-mounted wire former, which works on a similar levering principle while the wire is held between the metal stud and a small curved former.

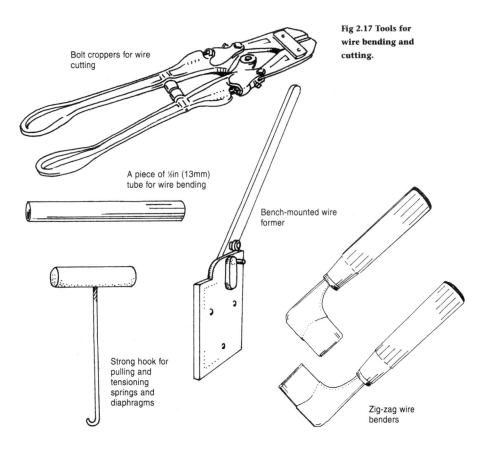

Bolt croppers for wire cutting

**Fig 2.17 Tools for wire bending and cutting.**

A piece of ½in (13mm) tube for wire bending

Bench-mounted wire former

Strong hook for pulling and tensioning springs and diaphragms

Zig-zag wire benders

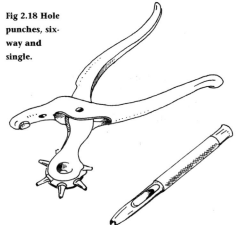

**Fig 2.18 Hole punches, six-way and single.**

## Hole punches (Fig 2.18)

The adjustable six-way hole punch cuts neat holes from about ½₁in (1.5mm) up to ¼in (6mm) in diameter in leather, plastics, fabrics, etc. Single punches for cutting holes in the centre of patterns, etc., are available in sizes ranging from ⅛–⅜in (3–10mm).

## Press-stud dies and punches (Fig 2.19)

These are used for fitting press-stud fasteners to tapes, cushions and detachable upholstery components (*see* page 37).

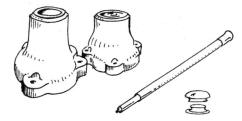

**Fig 2.19 (above) Press-stud dies and punch.**

**Fig 2.20 (right) Spring balance to weigh out fillings.**

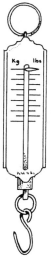

## Springing balances (Fig 2.20)

These are useful for checking and weighing fillings of all types. They should give the weight in kilograms and pounds so that comparisons can be made when necessary.

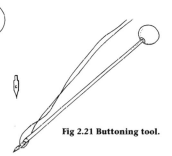

**Fig 2.21 Buttoning tool.**

## Buttoning tools (Fig 2.21)

These are designed for replacing upholstery buttons that have come loose or broken out. The loose dart forms an anchor inside the upholstered chair and a button can be retied on to the twine using a slip knot.

# Power Tools

## Electric staple gun (Fig 2.22)

This tool is relatively heavy and cumbersome. However, its firing power is good, provided it is held firmly against the work being fixed. On many models the nose length is rather short, limiting its use in confined spaces.

Regarding the staples, the gauge of wire used and the crown width will vary from one make to another (*see* pages 35–6). Length of staple leg ranges from ¼–⅜in (6–10mm).

Most staple guns are bottom loading, which means that the gun must be turned upside down and the magazine slid open for reloading.

General maintenance includes the following:

● Clean the magazine with a brush or compressed air.
● Protect the gun from damp conditions.

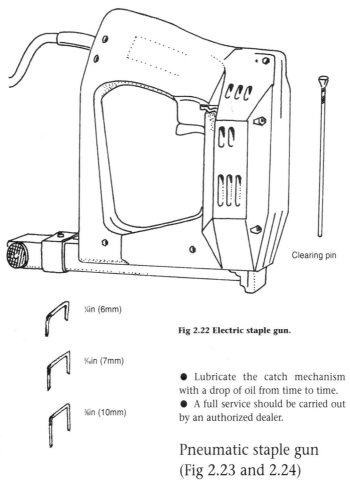

¼in (6mm)

⁵⁄₁₆in (7mm)

⅜in (10mm)

Clearing pin

**Fig 2.22 Electric staple gun.**

● Lubricate the catch mechanism with a drop of oil from time to time.
● A full service should be carried out by an authorized dealer.

## Pneumatic staple gun (Fig 2.23 and 2.24)

This is a compact and lightweight machine designed specifically for upholstery applications. It requires a minimum air pressure of 70psi. Pre-formed lengths of staples are bottom-loaded into the magazine at the base of the air gun. The firing action is relatively light and fast, mainly because of the simplicity of its action and its high power for weight ratio. Staple lengths for the gun range from ⅛–½in (3–13mm).

## Foam cutters (Fig 2.25 and 2.26)

For general foam cutting, shaping, chamfering etc., simple jigs formed with straight edges and pieces of timber can provide a variety of accurately cut foam parts (*see* pages 73–4). Blade lengths available are ¾in, 5⅛in, 8in and 12in (70mm, 130mm, 200mm and 305mm).

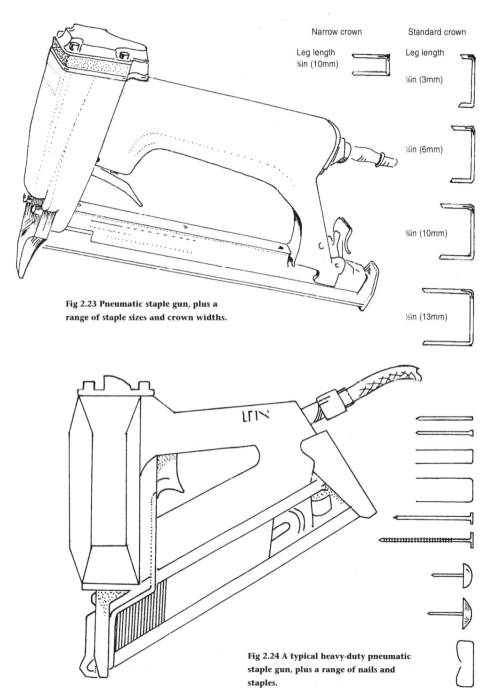

Narrow crown

Standard crown

Leg length
⅜in (10mm)

Leg length

⅛in (3mm)

¼in (6mm)

⅜in (10mm)

**Fig 2.23 Pneumatic staple gun, plus a
range of staple sizes and crown widths.**

½in (13mm)

**Fig 2.24 A typical heavy-duty pneumatic
staple gun, plus a range of nails and
staples.**

**Fig 2.25 Electric foam cutter.**

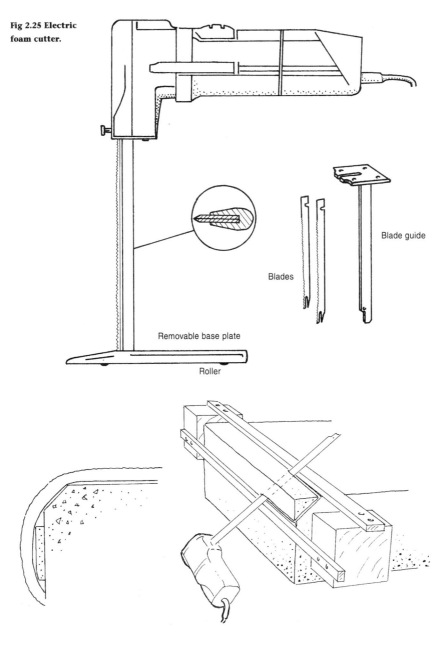

Blade guide

Blades

Removable base plate

Roller

**Fig 2.26 Cutting foam using a simple wooden jig made up from two end blocks and two thin straight battens. Jigs of this kind can be varied to suit the work and to make cutting precise and easily repeatable.**

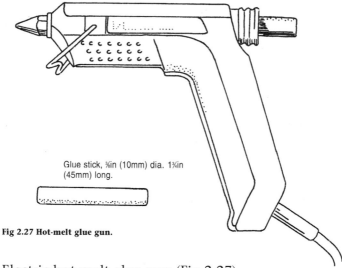

Glue stick, ⅜in (10mm) dia. 1¾in (45mm) long.

**Fig 2.27 Hot-melt glue gun.**

## Electric hot-melt glue gun (Fig 2.27)

This is a small, lightweight adhesive applicator. The heating element liquefies a solid glue stick which is pushed manually as glue is needed. Almost any materials in common use (excluding styrenes) may be bonded together using the correct adhesive (*see* page 40). The melted adhesive in the pistol is applied to the surface to be joined through the 1mm diameter nozzle. Some typical uses are: fabric to fabric, fabric to timber, fabric to metal, cardboard and millboard to wood frames, and some frame repairs.

## Electric drill (Fig 2.28)

The upholsterer will use the standard small electric drill, with two speeds and a ⅜in (10mm) chuck size. This can be used for a variety of drilling operations in wood and metal. Frame repairs and alterations, mainly in wood, using drills for screws and dowels, are the most common uses.

## Cordless drill/driver

The cordless drill/driver is able to drill holes quickly, as well as drive screws into furniture with reasonable ease.

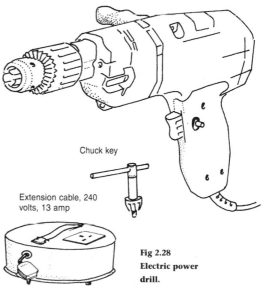

Chuck key

Extension cable, 240 volts, 13 amp

**Fig 2.28 Electric power drill.**

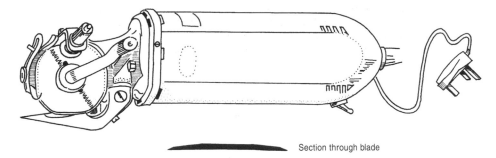

Section through blade

**Fig 2.29 Electric cloth cutter.**

## Electric cloth cutters (Fig 2.29)

The small hand-held electric cloth cutter is an alternative to hand shears, particularly if the cutting of covers includes regular cutting of long lengths of piping strips. It has a rotary cutting action and is fitted with a 1⅝in (40mm) blade capable of making very accurate straight and curved cuts.

# Machines

The preparation of materials for upholstery and bedding falls roughly into the following areas:

- Manufacture of springs and suspension.
- Conversion and fabrication of foams.
- Marking out and cutting of covers.
- Sewing and quilting of covers.
- Filling, buttoning and closing of cushions and foam units.

It is in these areas that machinery has been and will continue to be developed.

## Cloth inspection and measuring

Where large quantities of cloth are being bought and used, it is worth investing in a machine to help in quality control tests, labelling and measuring.

As the fabric is slowly unwound, it passes over a well-lit table surface, which allows clear visual inspection. The machine can be stopped at any point for flaws in the cloth to be marked or labelled at the selvedge. While the cloth travels from one side of the table to the other, a trumeter measuring device records the accurate length.

Machines of this type are available as horizontal or vertical tables. Most tables are fitted with electric cross cutters, which give the option of producing exact-cut lengths at any time should production necessitate.

Taking trouble to inspect cloth for faults before it is marked out or cut can have many advantages, not least the fact that goods cannot be returned once they are cut (see pages 123 and 145). Some common faults are: bad creasing, yarns drifting and not square to the selvedge, large knots, missing or broken yarns, distortion or bareness in pile fabrics, changes in density, and bad registration on printed fabrics.

## Cloth spreaders

When rolls of upholstery cover are required for marking and cutting, and a bulk or layered cutting system is being used, a cloth-spreading machine may be used to layer fabrics automatically on to the cutting table.

The operation of the machine, which is mounted on rails over the cutting table, commences when spreading begins at the right-hand end of the lay, and travels a predetermined length of the table to the left-hand end. Here it stops and the electrically operated cutter travels across the machine and cross cuts the lay end. The machine then returns to the right-hand end without spreading, clamps the fabric automatically and then continues with the selected laying sequence.

## Press cutting

A press-cutting machine consists of a series of shaped knives, or upstanding blades, which are set into a base board and form the surface of the cutting table. Fabrics are layered over the knives and clamped into position. When preparation is complete, the table is rolled under a hydraulic press, which stamps out the required shapes. It is usual to infill the areas around the blades with foam to the same height as the blades. This keeps the lay flat and also assists with removal of the cut parts.

## Industrial sewing machines (Fig 2.30)

The joining and quilting of covers and fabrics is one of the most important features of any piece of upholstery. For the small workshop carrying out a variety of work, one good machine of the right type and fitted with a range of accessories, will deal with almost all sewing operations. In industrial upholstery, the making up of sewn covers is generally broken down into a number of smaller operations, each dealt with by a specialized machine.

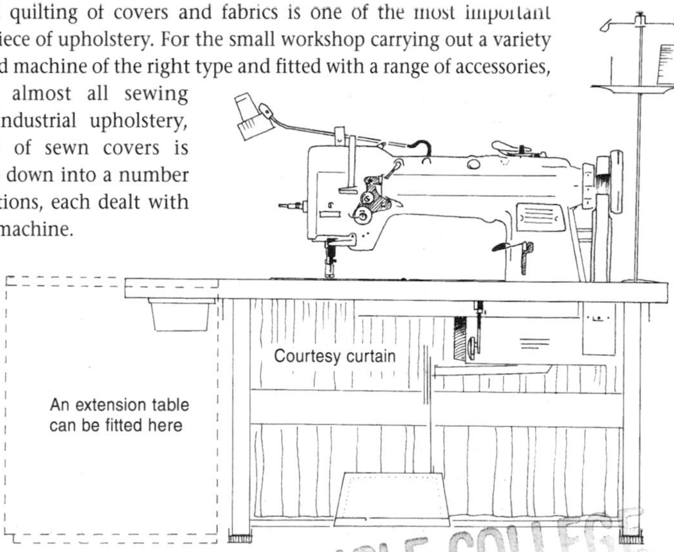

**Fig 2.30 Industrial sewing machine.**

Courtesy curtain

An extension table can be fitted here

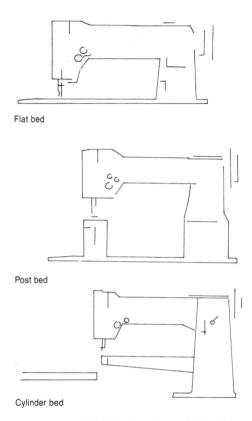

Flat bed

Post bed

Cylinder bed

**Fig 2.31 The three forms of lock-stitch machine.**

## Lock-stitch machines

The lock stitch is universal and is almost certainly the strongest seam stitch that can be produced (*see* page 89). Lock-stitch machines are produced as either single-needle or twin-needle models, and are available in three basic forms: flat bed, post bed and cylinder bed (Fig 2.31). A basic lock-stitch machine may have one of several different feed mechanisms (Fig 2.32):

**Drop feed** The fabric is fed forward by the moving feed dog, with the presser foot held on to the fabric by spring pressure. Needle movement is in a straight line up and down, with feed taking place when the needle is in the up position. This system is adequate for most lightweight applications.

**Compound or needle feed** Feed takes place with the needle in the down position, making a forward movement in unison with the feed dog. Adequate for light and medium upholstery covers.

**Compound feed with alternating presser** The presser foot – often called a walking foot – is a two-part mechanism arranged to alternate in pressing down of the fabric plies. Recommended for general and heavy upholstery, especially hide work, heavy tweeds and pile fabrics. Ideal for reupholstery.

**Differential feed** Basically a drop-feed mechanism with two feed dogs which can work at different rates, thus forming a gathering function in front of the needle. Recommended where a lot of puckering and gathering of fabrics is required, e.g. as a feature on chairs or cushions.

**Puller feeds** A powered roller puller can be fitted to most machines, mainly used for long runs of border making, zip insertion, and where different types of material are being quilted or laminated together, i.e. to assist in the straight sewing of difficult materials.

## Specialized lock-stitch machines

**Swing needle – zig-zag** These are basically lock-stitch and drop-feed machines, with the added feature of a swinging needle. They are sometimes used in soft

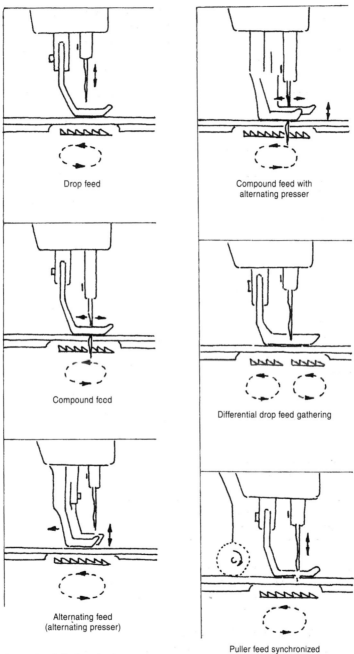

Drop feed

Compound feed with
alternating presser

Compound feed

Differential drop feed gathering

Alternating feed
(alternating presser)

Puller feed synchronized
with drop feed

**Fig 2.32 Work-feed mechanisms.**

furnishing; for example, the zig-zag seam is used where a decorative quilted effect is incorporated into a chair or cushion cover.

**Long-arm machines**   These are compound feed, lock-stitch types, with spoon- or boat-shaped presser feet and a long machine head arm. They are essential when producing fluted and quilted panels in quantity (*see* page 144).

## Chain-stitch machines
These are either single- or two-thread machines. Their advantage over lock-stitch machines is that the stitches are simply formed by the needle thread and need no underthread or bobbin (*see* page 89); therefore the machines can be run continuously with no stops for bobbin change. This makes them well suited to certain mass-production situations e.g. the preparation of sewn parts, or pre-sewing, with components such as zipped borders and piping, all of which will later be sewn again into made up covers. However, the seam itself does not compare in strength or tightness to the lock stitch, and if it is put under great strain for any length of time, then gaping and seam-opening problems occur.

## Overedge machines (Fig 2.33)
These may be two-, three-, or four-thread and single- or two-needle. The stitch is basically a chain stitch with a looper and a needle producing the overlock, a second needle providing the safety stitch alongside the overlocking one. They are used to make cut edges fray-proof, adding to seam strength where slip covers, arm caps and cushion covers are removable.

## Specialist sewing machines
The need for specialized sewing has grown from the part-production principle where an upholstery cover, once produced completely by one operator, is now broken down into a series of smaller operations carried out by several people on a variety of machines. The product progresses from a number of prepared components, to final assembly by one machinist on a standard lock-stitch machine.

**Quilters**   Single or multi-needle; will produce flat sewn panels ready for insertion into a mattress or chair.

**Twin-head boxing or cushion-boxing machines**   These produce boxed cushions (*see* page 118) and covers by joining border strips to top and bottom panels simultaneously, and finish the edges plain sewn or with piped or ruched seams.

**Profile seamers**   These sew together an almost unlimited range of sub-assemblies quickly and accurately. Using an autojig system the machine stitches and trims one or two plies of fabric to the predetermined shape.

**Automatic straight seamers**   These have synchronized puller feeds on top and bottom, a double-chain-stitch head, thread cutters and monitors. They are useful where long straight seams are required, such as lengthening or widening of cloth panels, applying lines and flies, and pre-sewing before shaping.

**Continuous zippers**   These are usually two- or four-needle, and may be chain

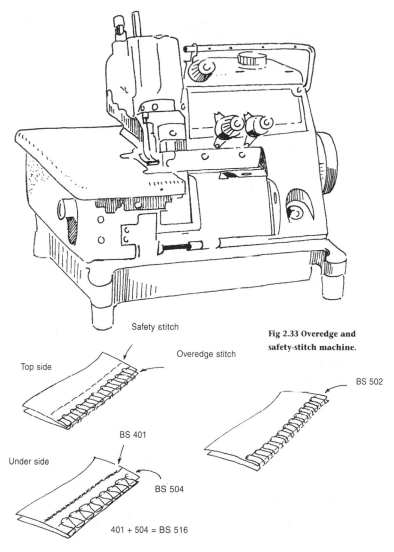

Safety stitch

Overedge stitch

**Fig 2.33 Overedge and safety-stitch machine.**

Top side

BS 502

BS 401

Under side

BS 504

401 + 504 = BS 516

stitch or lock stitch. They are designed for the fast production of zipped components and continuous zipped borders.

## Button-making and buttoning machines (Figs 2.34 and 2.35)

The button-making process requires discs of fabric to be cut to suit the size of the die, followed by the clamping of the upper and lower parts together with the cover moulded around the upper or dome surface. There are now semi- and fully-

fully-automatic button-making machines, normally pneumatic with electronic functions, which can produce from 600 to 3,000 buttons of any type per hour.

Button-fastening machines use a combination of pneumatic power and steel frames to locate, hold and compress a piece of upholstery. All types of anchor or open-hook buttons and tufts may be used, and fastening can be deep or shallow. The process of buttoning through can either be done automatically using cylinder-powered needles to pierce the upholstery in one single stroke, or manually by using a hand needle.

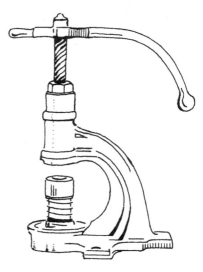

**Fig 2.34 Bench-mounted, button-making fly press.**

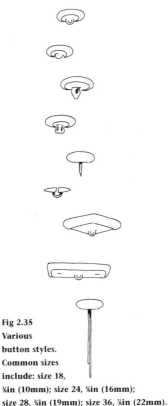

**Fig 2.35 Various button styles. Common sizes include: size 18, ⅜in (10mm); size 24, ⅝in (16mm); size 28, ¾in (19mm); size 36, ⅞in (22mm).**

## Cushion filling by machine

There are three types of automatic cushion filler, which all compress and eject the filling in different ways. The box-ram-type pneumatic cushion filler uses compressed air to squash the fillings down to the size of the cover opening, after which a ram pushes the filling into the cover while it is held over the mouth of the box. The arm-type compression cushion filler has eight tubular steel arms which move together to compress the interior. The cover is then pulled over and the arms are retracted leaving the filled case ready for closing. The conveyor-type cushion filler operates vertically, compressing almost any type of filling inside the cabinet. Ejection into the cushion cover is by means of small conveyors and rollers pushing the interior upwards into the ready-made case.

# Fixings and Fittings

## Tacks (Fig 2.36)

Cut-steel, blued tacks are made in four sizes and in two grades: fine and improved. Fine tacks are the standard types used for most upholstery fixing work. Sizes are given as the overall length and are ¼in, ⅜in, ½in and ⅝in (6mm, 10mm, 13mm and 16mm).

This range will serve for most purposes, except when a very loose woven material is to be fixed, or when a substantial fixing is needed through several heavy layers. The improved range of sizes are of slightly heavier gauge, and have larger heads. Many upholsterers use improved tacks for webbing and hessian work and keep fine tacks for scrims, covers and general fixings. ¼in (6mm) sizes need only be kept in very small amounts, as they are useful only for very fine work, or on thin plywood panels.

For very long fixings, fine tacks are available at ¾in and 1in (19mm and 25mm). All sizes are available in small 500g and large 10kg boxes.

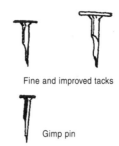

Fine and improved tacks

Gimp pin

**Fig 2.36 Fine and improved tacks, and a gimp pin (below).**

## Gimp pins

The gimp pin is a fine-cut, coloured steel pin used traditionally for the fixing of gimps, braids and fringes. It is also very useful as a fine fixing in many areas of upholstery, particularly for finishing, and as a first fixing before bandings or brass nails are applied.

Gimp pin sizes are ⅜in and ½in (10mm and 13mm) and pins are available in white, black, fawn, grey, yellow, red, green, blue and brown.

## Staples (Fig 2.37)

### Wire staples

Bright-steel or galvanized steel ⅝in (15mm) wire staples are used in upholstery mostly for the holding of springs on to timber frames, and for edge wires, and the occasional fixing of lightweight tension springs.

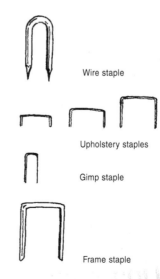

Wire staple

Upholstery staples

Gimp staple

Frame staple

**Fig 2.37 Staples.**

## Upholstery staples

An efficient, fast and very clean industrial fastener, which has replaced the tack in commercial upholstery. The upholstery staple has a crown width of approximately ⅜in (10mm) and is made in five leg lengths: ⅛in, ¼in, ⅜in ½in and ¹¹⁄₁₆in (3mm, 6mm, 10mm, 13mm and 17mm). They are produced for use in manual, electric or pneumatic staple guns. An average box contains 10,000 staples in pre-formed magazine lengths. The standard size staple is available in a silver or with the crown surface painted black.

## Gimp staples

These staples have a narrow crown about 4mm wide, and, when fired into fabrics, are almost hidden. They are available in several different painted colours, and are used as final fixings on cover and trimmings. Because of the narrow crown width, a special gun is needed to fire this type of staple.

## Framing staples

Heavy-duty stapling is now common in assembly of chair frames, and for the fixing of springs and spring units (*see* pages 75–82). These jobs call for staples of a heavy gauge with leg lengths up to 2in (50mm).

# Nails (Fig 2.38)

## Clout nails

These are bright-steel wire nails with a large head, made in three leg-length sizes: ¾in, 1in and 1¼in (19mm, 25mm and 32mm). Their main function in upholstery is the fixing of springs and spring units. They are extremely strong and their large head provides a good sound fixing.

## Bright-steel jagged nails

A smaller slimmer version of the clout nail, but with a jagged leg design, which gives good holding in timber frames. Jagged nails are ¾in (19mm) long and are used particularly in spring fixing where movement of components can cause the loosening of fixing nails (e.g. the spring clips used to hold sinuous wire [zig-zag] springs).

## Serrated clout tacks

The clout tack is a blued-steel heavy tack, with a very large head and jagged or serrated leg. Designed as an alternative to the clout nail, they have very good holding properties similar to the jagged nail, and are used in the springing area of upholstery production. Length: 1in (25mm).

Clout nail            Jagged nail            Clout tack

**Fig 2.38 Nails.**

## Upholstery nails (Fig 2.39)

This is a range of decorative nails which has been used by the upholsterer for well over 250 years. These days the upholstery nail is only used as a decoration and finish in traditional and reproduction work (*see* pages 126–7). The range and design of nail heads is very wide, and selection must be made with care.

Standard size nails are about ⅜in (10mm) diameter with a ¾in (19mm) leg length. Surface treatment of the domed heads can vary from plain brass to intricate design, embossed pattern and enamelled paint finishes. British and French nails are particularly good, having a steel leg and a fancy raised head.

## Press studs (Fig 2.40)

The press stud is used for fixing upholstery covers down and holding them in place, while at the same time allowing for easy removal at a later date. It can be used to fix fabric to fabric, fabric to wood or metal, and fabrics or straps to lightweight board materials.

The component parts are located and hammered together, producing male and female locations. The female base components can be screwed or bolted to timber or metal frames. The strength of the joint produced depends largely on the number of press studs used in an area.

Should press studs be used on some lightweight cloths, then reinforcement will probably be necessary: fold an edge several times, or put in a stiffener such as canvas, scrim or a non-woven lining, before the studs are fitted.

Most upholsterers use the standard silver chrome or nickel-plated press stud, but they are also available in enamelled colours.

**Fig 2.39 Upholstery nails.**

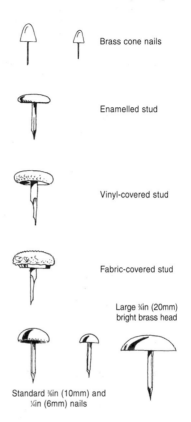

Brass cone nails

Enamelled stud

Vinyl-covered stud

Fabric-covered stud

Large ¾in (20mm) bright brass head

Standard ⅜in (10mm) and ¼in (6mm) nails

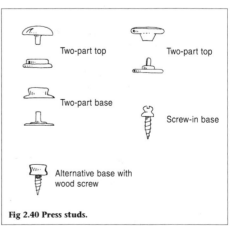

Two-part top

Two-part top

Two-part base

Screw-in base

Alternative base with wood screw

**Fig 2.40 Press studs.**

## Ventilators (Fig 2.41)

The ventilator is used in cushion making and mattress borders to allow a flow of air into and out of a confined space. They should be fitted in cushion making when non-breathable coverings (e.g. hides or vinyls) are used, but are always fitted to mattresses, whatever the covering. Vents should be fitted at the backs or along the borders of coverings where they will not be too obvious.

**Fig 2.41 Ventilators**

Brass ventilator and base

There are two types generally available: the brass ventilator, which requires tooling to fit it to a fabric, and the plastic vent, which can simply be fixed into a pre-cut hole by hand. Average size: ¾in (19mm).

Plastic vent

Press-on clip

## Eyelets (Fig 2.42)

Eyelets are fittings which tend to be used in modern upholstery. They are often needed in leather and canvas work and can also be used for ventilation. They range in size from the small lace-hole type up to 1in (25mm) in diameter. The tools required to press eyelets into a fabric are fairly simple and are usually supplied with a pack of eyelet parts. An eyelet is made up of a top and a base ring. These are fitted together with the fabric in between and hammered together. Once made, the fixing is permanent, so care should be taken to ensure correct positioning before a hole is cut.

The assembled vent

Small one-piece eyelet

Eyelets can be fitted where a permanent hole is needed, as a means of taking cord, elastic or lace through a cover. They can also be used effectively as rivets to finish or strengthen a joint, or at the end of a heavy seam.

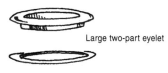

Large two-part eyelet

**Fig 2.42 Eyelets.**

## Facing fixings (Fig 2.43)

These are used to fix and hold plywood facings on to chair arm fronts. The correct hole size allows for a tight push fit.

Facing fixing, black plastic, ¾–1⅝in (20–40mm)

## Glues (Fig 2.44)

### General purpose contact adhesives
Contact adhesives are normally applied to both surfaces to be bonded, allowed to dry for 10–15 minutes, and the bond made by applying pressure.

Panel and facing fixing, sprung metal

**Dunlop S758** A versatile, high strength contact adhesive ideal for bonding a wide range of

**Fig 2.43 Facing fixings.**

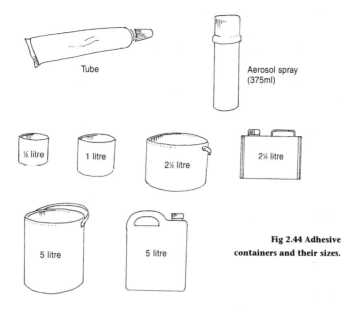

Fig 2.44 Adhesive
containers and their sizes.

materials, including wood, rigid plastics, GRP (glass-reinforced plastic) and rubber. Container sizes: 5l, 1l, 500ml.

SN1314   A nonflammable version of S758 for use in areas where flammable solvents are prohibited. Container sizes: 5l, 1l, 500ml.

S1358   Similar to S758 but ideal where heat resistance is required up to 100°C.

Dunlop Powerfix   A solvent-free, non-drip, contact adhesive which is water based. Changes in colour from white to clear when ready for bonding. Exhibits very long open time and bonds can be made up to several days after coating. Container sizes: 5l, 500ml, 250ml, 120ml, 30ml.

Dunlop Easy Spray   Produced in an aerosol can, this is a high-tack, multi-purpose adhesive. Adjustable nozzle gives variable spray width. Ideal for upholstery work. Adheres well to wood and metal and has good heat resistance. Bonds can be made after 30 seconds or up to 30 minutes. Can size: 370g.

## Foam bonding and textile adhesives

Dunlop L107 solution   Bonds latex and polyurethane foams, scrim, hessian and leather, to wood, chipboard and hardboard. Applied by brush or scraper and very clean to use. Can sizes: 5l, 1l, 500ml.

SN1789   Nonflammable, sprayable, foam-building adhesive. Bonds natural and synthetic foam, as well as furnishing fabrics, hessian and polyester fibre fillings, allowing substrates to be bonded almost immediately. Excellent coverage, giving clear, flexible film. Container sizes: 25l, 5l.

**A1020**   Water-based adhesive for bonding textiles and paper. A quick-sealing latex adhesive for textile bonding, especially carpet seaming and edging. Also used for paper, cardboard and yarn splicing. Dries to a clear film. Can size: 5l.

**S1588**   PVC adhesive for flexible plastics. Specially developed for bonding unsupported plasticized PVC and polyurethane materials. Bonds to metal, has good oil resistance and is applied by brush or scraper. Can size: 5l.

**Dunlop Extra Strong PVA Wood Glue**   Gives high-strength bonds on soft woods and hard woods, plywood and chipboard. Dries to a clear film. Sizes: 5l, 500ml, 250ml, 125ml.

## Thinners and cleaners

**Dunlop T559**   General-purpose thinner and cleaner for use with most synthetic adhesives. Container sizes: 5l, 2½l.

**TN1239**   Nonflammable; for use with nonflammable solvent adhesives. Container sizes: 5l, 2½l.

**Copydex fabric adhesive**   A white fabric-to-fabric contact adhesive. Ideal for trimmings and edge sealing of fabrics. Container sizes: 5l, 1l, 500ml. Brush included in small sizes.

**JDW heavy-duty, aerosol-spray, nonflammable contact adhesive**   Ideal for general upholstery work. Container size: 365ml.

**UHU clear contact adhesive**   Good, general-purpose contact fabric adhesive. Ideal for the permanent application of trimmings. May be applied to one surface only, with quick bond after light pressure.

**Hot-melt adhesive**   For use with electric, hot-melt glue guns (*see* page 27). A clear adhesive producing an instant bond when applied to one surface. Glue sticks should be selected to suit variable applications. Available in 1kg and 500g packs.

## Fabric and leather bonding to timber substrates

**PVA wood glues**   A white, ready-mixed, water-based adhesive which dries to a clear film. Works well for this purpose when thinned by watering down: four parts glue to one part water. A water-resistant PVA emulsion which has an open time of 4–10 minutes. Surplus adhesive should be removed with a damp cloth and tools cleaned with fresh water.

**Heavy-duty wallpaper paste**   Mixed to medium/heavy viscosity as per the manufacturer's instructions. A water paste in powder form which is ready for use 3–5 minutes after mixing. Easy slip properties allow for movement and adjustment of materials. Surplus adhesive should be removed with a damp cloth. Ideal for fabric and leather inlays and pinched fabric effects.

# Chair Frame Materials, Construction and Design

The requirements of an upholstered frame are an ability to withstand many different kinds of pressure, while remaining strong and supportive with some flexibility. It must be dimensionally stable, and able to withstand the pulling and straining forces imposed by webbings, suspension materials and springing systems. Timbers must have good holding properties for screwing, stapling and nailing, and must be easily machined, so that accurate, well-fitted joints can be produced. Dimensions and proportions are other considerations which are closely linked with good design.

# Materials and Joints

## Timbers for chair frames (Fig 3.1)

Beech, birch, ash and mahogany are the main woods used for frame making. Ramin and sapele are two other hardwoods which have the required qualities. All timbers used should be free from defects, wild grain or irregular surfaces, and not be prone

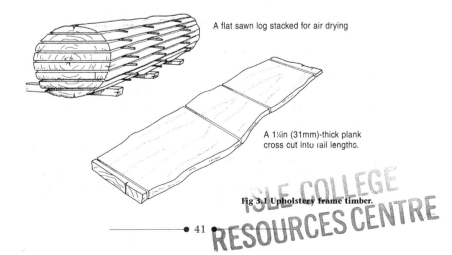

A flat sawn log stacked for air drying

A 1¼in (31mm)-thick plank cross cut into rail lengths.

**Fig 3.1 Upholstery frame timber.**

to softness, lifting grain or splitting. Suitable timbers are air- and kiln-dried to controlled moisture contents in the range of 9 to 12%. All the above-mentioned timbers work, joint and glue well, and have excellent holding properties.

Softwoods can be used (and are used in Scandinavian countries) for upholstery frames, provided that the fixings are heavier and the upholstery techniques are not dependent on conventional tacking and stapling.

## Board Materials

Various lightweight board materials, produced from timber, make up a large percentage of the content of modern frames. They are used to line upholstery chair frames and to support the filling in the modern chair. The boards do the job traditionally done by webbings and hessian. However, because of their strength, they are often used to help strengthen a chair frame, either as main structures or as linings and stiffeners, using the principle of box construction. The four board materials used in upholstery frames are plywood, hardboard, millboard and chipboard. They are all manufactured in 8 x 4ft (2.4 x 1.2m) sheets.

### Plywood

Although the most expensive, plywood is probably the most versatile and strongest of the boards used. It is available in a wide range of types and thicknesses from ½in to ¾in (1–20mm). However, most commonly used in upholstery framing is thin plywood, ⅛–¼in (3–6mm) thick. These thinner sheets can easily be bent or formed to provide large curved surfaces. Plywood is also used for stiffening and reinforcing frames, as gussets, corner blocks and linings.

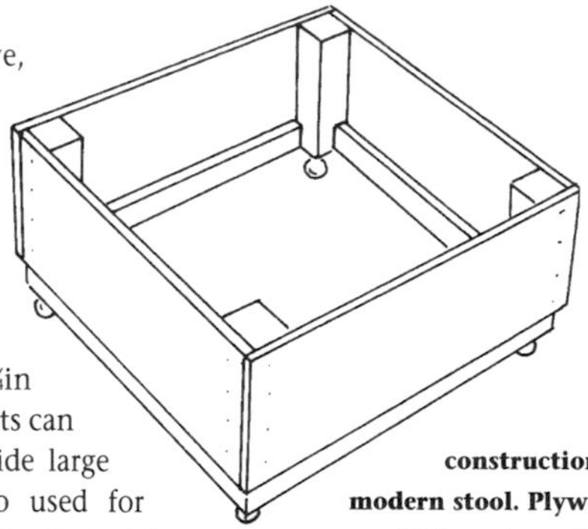

**Fig 3.2 Box-construction frame of a modern stool. Plywood, MDF or chipboard may be used for a carcass of this type.**

### Hardboard and millboard

These are generally used to line and infill upholstery frames, particularly on back rests, inside arms and platform fronts. Thicknesses vary from ¼in (6mm) down to very thin millboards at ¹⁄₁₆in (1.5mm). The most common thicknesses in upholstery framing are ³⁄₁₆in (5mm) for hardboard, and ½–⅛in (2–3mm) for millboard. Both boards are lightweight, flexible and make good supports and stiffeners for wood and metal structures. They are also very dense materials and have good staple- and nail-holding properties. Millboard, a dark grey or black high-density

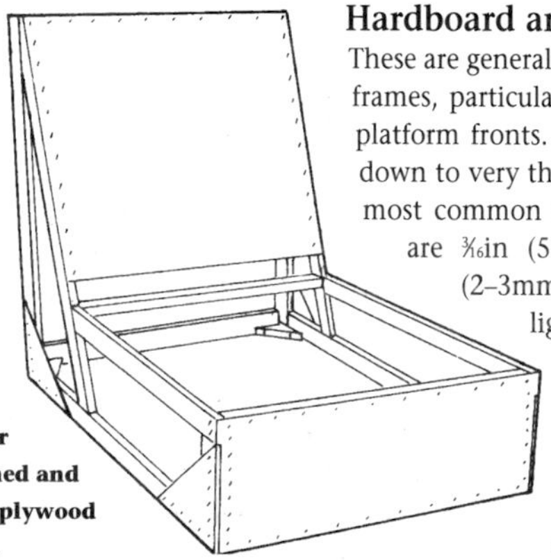

**Fig 3.3 Unit frame: a timber chair frame lined and stiffened with plywood and millboard.**

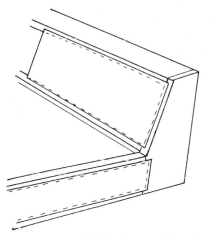

**Fig 3.4 Inside arm and seat front lined with millboard.**

fibreboard, is pliable enough to be stapled or pinned around shaped framing. Layers of hardboard and millboard can be laminated together to produce shaped components.

## Chipboard and medium-density fibreboard (MDF)

These are generally much thicker and heavier than the other types, and if used in large amounts in a frame there is a noticeable increase in weight. However, where a strong board of good thickness and strength is required, these can be ideal. Wings, arms and seat fronts are often produced using these boards. Thicknesses range from ¼–1³⁄₁₆in (6–30mm) for use in furniture.

All board materials should be used with the recommended jointing and fixing techniques so that they improve and strengthen rather than merely cheapen the frame-making process.

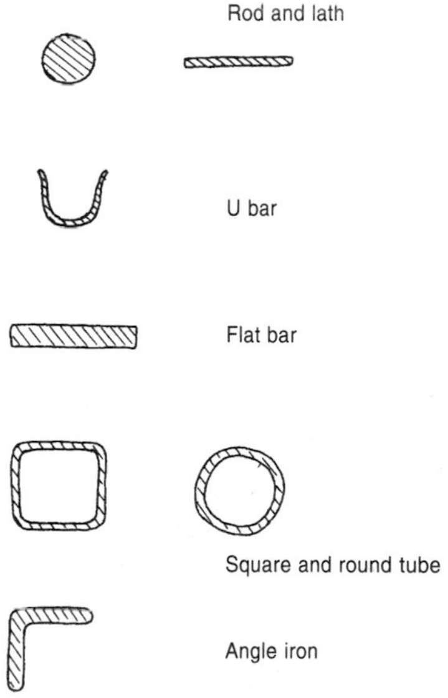

## Metals (Fig 3.5)

Steel in the form of rod, bar and tube, is welded and bolted to produce upholstery frames. Angle iron, U-bar and steel lath are also used to some extent. It is sometimes simpler and less costly to produce a frame in metal rather than in timber, particularly if compound shapes and curves are involved in the design. Square and round-section tube are the most common sections used for frame making. Their excellent strength/weight ratio makes them ideal framing materials. Where necessary, timber base frames or boards can be added to provide easy fixing for the upholstery. Metal frames require a different approach to upholstery design and application. Clips and adhesives are used as fixings, and tailored jacket covers can be clipped or zipped to hold them in place.

Rod and lath

U bar

Flat bar

Square and round tube

Angle iron

**Fig 3.5 Metal sections.**

## Plastics (Fig 3.6)

There are three plastic materials used in the manufacture of upholstered seating – GRP (glass-reinforced polyester resin), expanded polystyrene and rigid polyurethane foam. All are rigid plastics and have to be moulded to produce frames or frame components. Plastics are suited to low- or high-volume production but are seldom used for one-off pieces of upholstery.

## Joints (Fig 3.7)

The mortise and tenon joint is a traditional timber frame joint suitable for all types of frame structure. An average tenon thickness is ⅜in (10mm), and its length will vary depending on rail dimensions.

The dowel joint is the other regularly used joint in timber frame construction. A dowel diameter of ⅜in (10mm) is average for most main joints, and length of dowel depends on the dimensions of the rail. Dowel joints may incorporate one, two or three dowels, again depending on rail size.

Where it is important to stop a rail from twisting in use, for example a stuffing rail, then joints are housed as well as dowelled. The lap joint and the finger joint are both used extensively to lengthen rails and as corner joints. They are both machine-made joints and lend themselves well to modern frame production.

Stapled and glued butt joints are an effective alternative to the other more conventional joints, particularly if gussets and stiffeners are used as braces.

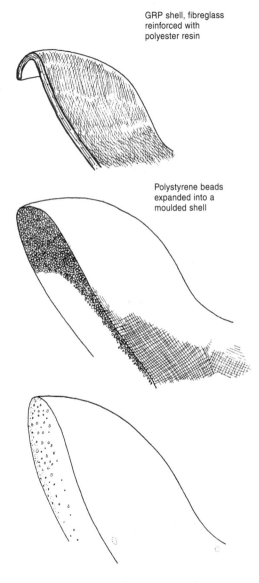

GRP shell, fibreglass reinforced with polyester resin

Polystyrene beads expanded into a moulded shell

Rigid polyurethane foam shell

**Fig 3.6 Plastic materials used in the manufacture of upholstered seating.**

**Fig 3.7 Joints used in timber
frame making**

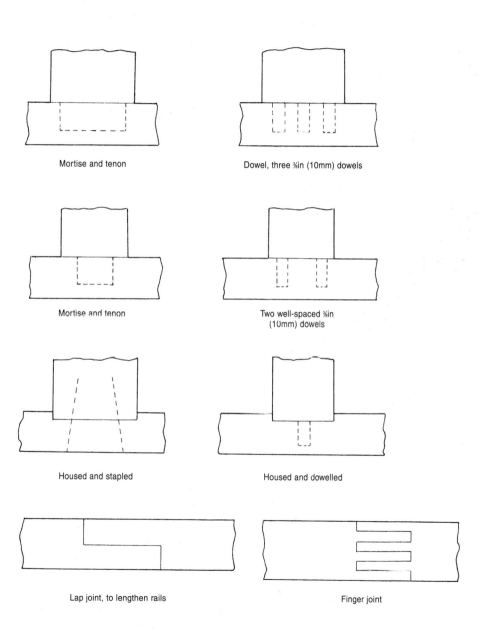

Mortise and tenon

Dowel, three ⅜in (10mm) dowels

Mortise and tenon

Two well-spaced ⅜in
(10mm) dowels

Housed and stapled

Housed and dowelled

Lap joint, to lengthen rails

Finger joint

# Construction

There are three basic upholstered chair frame constructions: fixed mono frames, KD (knock-down) frames and unit frames. A fixed mono frame is a complete free-standing structure, made and assembled and finished ready for upholstery. It is made up from machined timber and board piece parts and may have elements of metal and plastic.

A KD frame is manufactured in sections, with assembly taking place after the sections have been upholstered. KD fittings of various kinds are used to hold the sections together. This method of making is designed principally for mass production and involves repetition work on a large scale. Although basic materials costs may be higher, speed and uniformity of production result from the breaking down of the product into small sections.

The unit frame is based on the principle of versatile seating, which can be arranged to suit different room situations. The units are usually either standard seats or corner seats, with a facility for arm supports to be added. Individual units may be free-standing or bolted together.

**Fig 3.8 Conventional chair frame construction using solid timber**

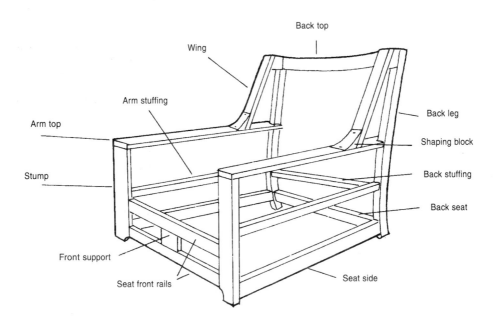

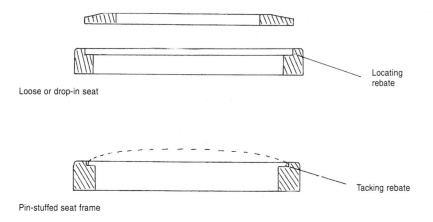

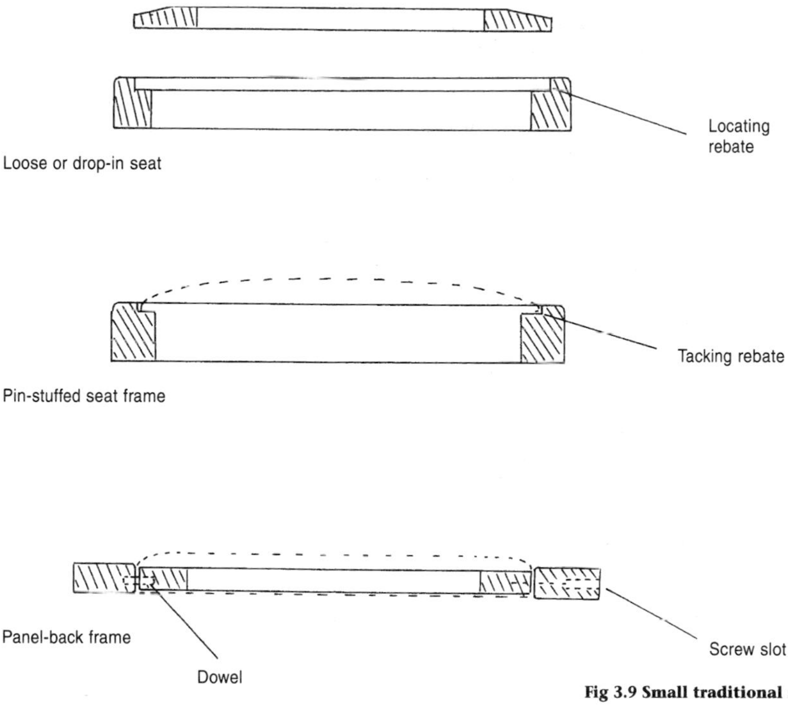

Loose or drop-in seat

Locating rebate

Pin-stuffed seat frame

Tacking rebate

Panel-back frame

Dowel

Screw slot

**Fig 3.9 Small traditional seat and back frames for dining, desk and reading chairs.**

**Fig 3.10 Part front elevation of a settee frame.**

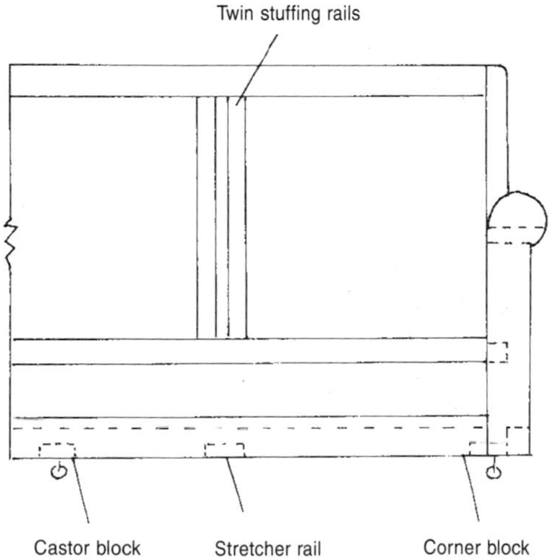

Twin stuffing rails

Castor block    Stretcher rail    Corner block

Three types of dowel

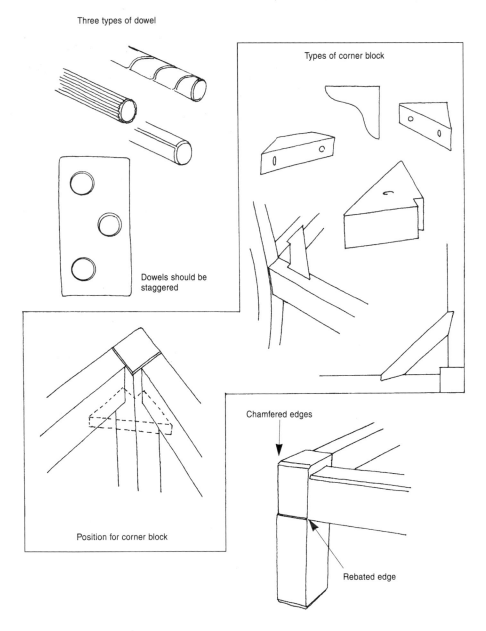

Types of corner block

Dowels should be staggered

Position for corner block

Chamfered edges

Rebated edge

**Fig 3.11 Dowel joints and corner blocks.**

**Fig 3.12 Examples of shapes and supports. Inset: a peg-fixed seat frame.**

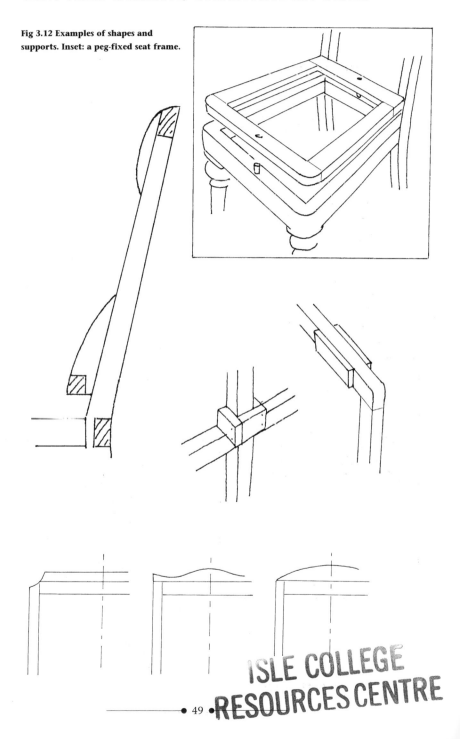

**Fig 3.13 Some examples of the use of plywood in seating and box constructions.**

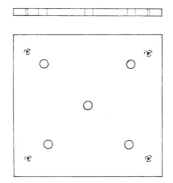

Plywood seat

Fixing is by means of four ¼in (6mm) tee nuts

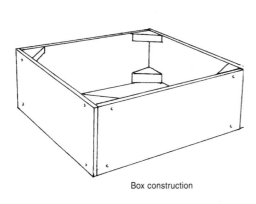

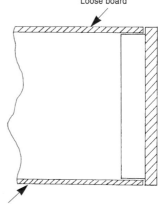

Loose board

Box construction

Fixed bottom

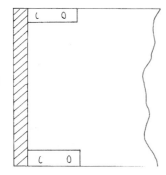

Close-up section of the above

Box construction with a loose seat board that acts both as a support for the seat and a lid to the storage area below

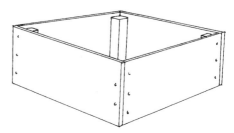

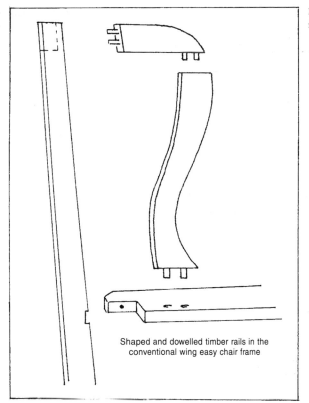

**Fig 3.14 Wing frame alternatives.**

Shaped and dowelled timber rails in the conventional wing easy chair frame

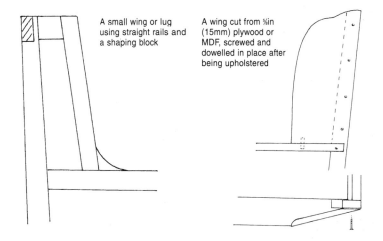

A small wing or lug using straight rails and a shaping block

A wing cut from ⅝in (15mm) plywood or MDF, screwed and dowelled in place after being upholstered

**Fig 3.15 Some variations of scroll and C-scroll frame work. Access to seat rail fixing is vital so that upholstery material can be positioned easily. All joints may be dowel, or seat rails could be tenoned into the main uprights.**

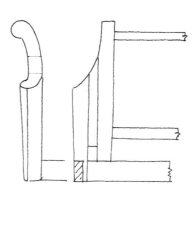

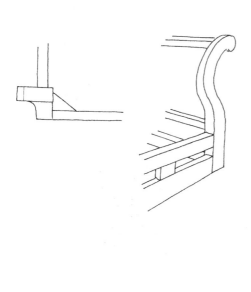

The set-back scroll produced by planting on to straight uprights or by cutting directly from the plank

A typical example of C scroll framing construction

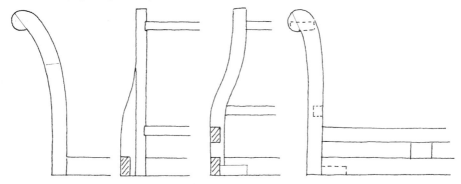

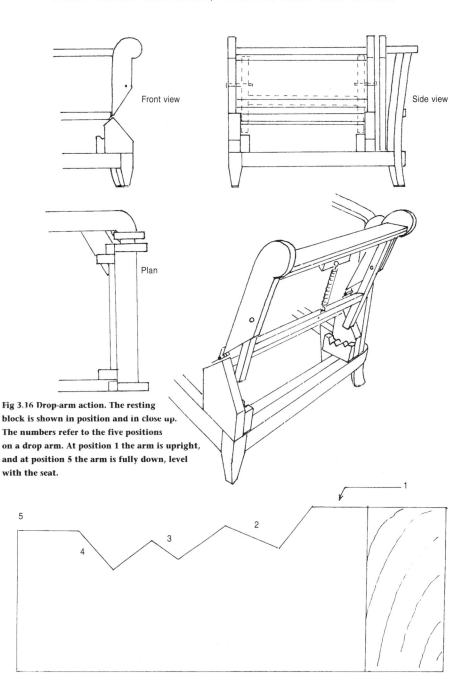

Front view

Side view

Plan

Fig 3.16 Drop-arm action. The resting
block is shown in position and in close up.
The numbers refer to the five positions
on a drop arm. At position 1 the arm is upright,
and at position 5 the arm is fully down, level
with the seat.

**Fig 3.17 Stretchers.**

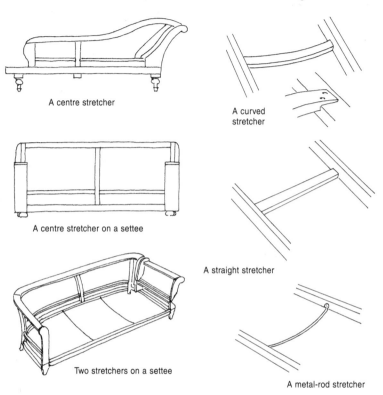

A centre stretcher

A curved stretcher

A centre stretcher on a settee

A straight stretcher

Two stretchers on a settee

A metal-rod stretcher

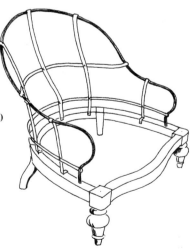

**Fig 3.18 A Victorian iron-back chair in which ⅜in (10mm) rod and ¾in (20mm) lath are combined to produce strong, flexible frames with interesting curving lines.**

# Fittings

## KD fittings

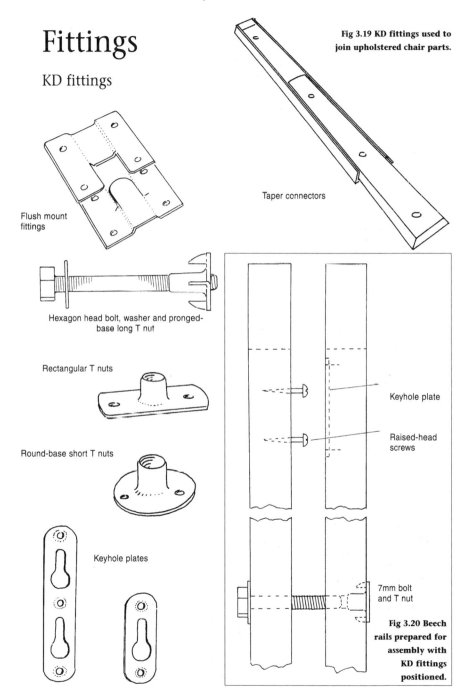

**Fig 3.19 KD fittings used to join upholstered chair parts.**

Flush mount fittings

Taper connectors

Hexagon head bolt, washer and pronged-base long T nut

Rectangular T nuts

Round-base short T nuts

Keyhole plates

Keyhole plate

Raised-head screws

7mm bolt and T nut

**Fig 3.20 Beech rails prepared for assembly with KD fittings positioned.**

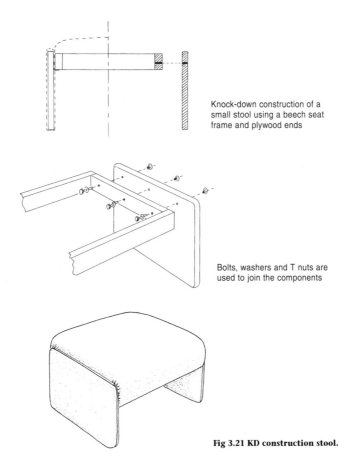

Knock-down construction of a
small stool using a beech seat
frame and plywood ends

Bolts, washers and T nuts are
used to join the components

**Fig 3.21 KD construction stool.**

## Castors and glides

Castors are fitted to chairs, settees and beds principally to facilitate movement. They are selected on the basis of the furniture's size, weight and design, as well as its function and loading. Most types are graded by the size of the wheel. Style, colour and fixings are equally important factors when choosing new castors for reproduction work and as replacements on period furniture. Fig 3.22 shows a range of the most common types of modern and traditional castors.

Glides and silencers (Fig 3.23) are very often fitted as alternatives to castors on contemporary furniture. These may be rigid or revolving, and are sometimes height-adjustable. In most cases glides or silencers are purely functional and are fitted so that they are not seen.

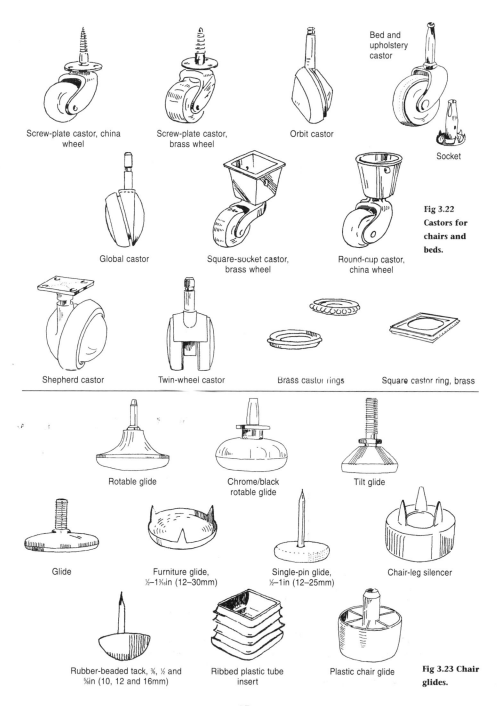

Screw-plate castor, china wheel

Screw-plate castor, brass wheel

Orbit castor

Bed and upholstery castor

Socket

Global castor

Square-socket castor, brass wheel

Round-cup castor, china wheel

**Fig 3.22 Castors for chairs and beds.**

Shepherd castor

Twin-wheel castor

Brass castor rings

Square castor ring, brass

Rotable glide

Chrome/black rotable glide

Tilt glide

Glide

Furniture glide, ½–1⅜in (12–30mm)

Single-pin glide, ½–1in (12–25mm)

Chair-leg silencer

Rubber-beaded tack, ⅜, ½ and ⅝in (10, 12 and 16mm)

Ribbed plastic tube insert

Plastic chair glide

**Fig 3.23 Chair glides.**

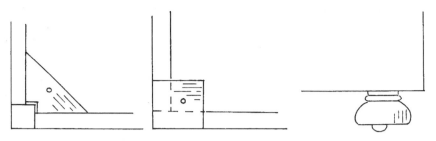

**Fig 3.24 (above)Fixing blocks and feet for castors and glides. Direction of grain is important.**

**Fig 3.25 (below) Dimensions and proportions for seating.**

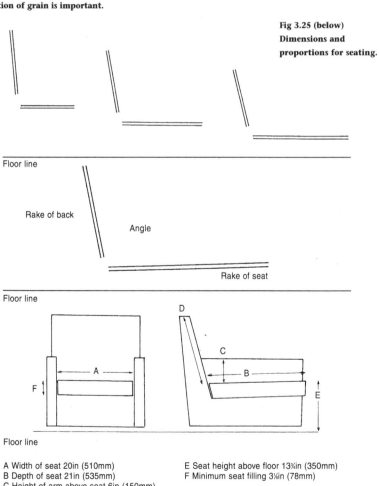

Floor line

Rake of back

Angle

Rake of seat

Floor line

Floor line

A Width of seat 20in (510mm)
B Depth of seat 21in (535mm)
C Height of arm above seat 6in (150mm)
D Height of back above seat to give head rest 22in (560mm)

E Seat height above floor 13¾in (350mm)
F Minimum seat filling 3⅛in (78mm)

# Upholstery through the Ages

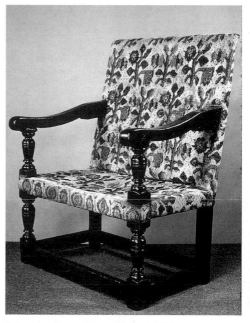

Oak and turkey-work armchair, c. 1640.

Late 18th-century wing chair with a damask covering.

William IV day bed buttoned in blue damask.

English Bergère armchair, mahogany, c. 1893.

# Frames and Joints

A close up of the iron work on a Victorian iron-back chair showing the stuffing rod fitted through the uprights.

A well-made chesterfield settee frame with drop-end action.

A handsome, newly restored Georgian wing armchair frame on mahogany cabriole legs, ready for the upholsterer.

A modern beech frame chaise longue which uses KD construction and separates into three main parts.

# Webbings

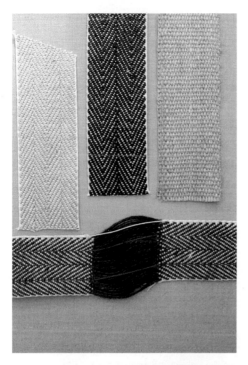

A webbed seat three by three
interwoven.

Clockwise from top left:
brown-and-white (undyed) webbing;
black-and-white English webbing;
plain weave 100% jute webbing;
black-dyed warp threads, two red warps
and white cotton edge.

Black-and-white English webbing
interlaced on an armchair seat.

# Springs and Foams

A traditional cane edge lashed
and bent to the seat front shape.

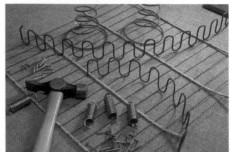

A range of traditional and modern springs including
hour-glass springs and zig-zag tension spring

A sprung and lashed bible-front
seat in a large armchair; the four
front springs have yet to be fixed
in place.

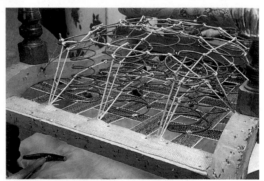

Urethane foam components ready for assembly and fabrication.

# Machines and Sewing

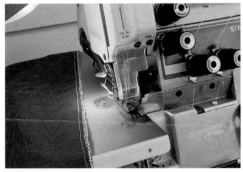

A four-thread overlock machine with the twin needles clearly visible.

A heavy-duty vertical blade cloth cutter.

A cylinder-bed machine.

A heavy-duty single-needle lock-stitch machine fitted with an alternating presser (walking foot).

# Trimmings

**Tufts, gimps, braids and fringes.**

A range of upholstery cords.

A contrast cord on a 19th-century chesterfield.

**Tufts, buttons and cords.**

# Covers
and Fabrics

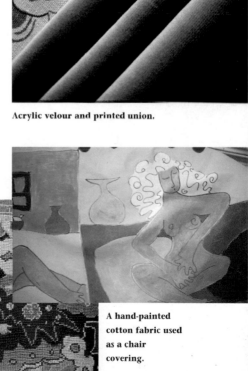

Acrylic velour and printed union.

A fine reproduction of an old print.

A hand-painted
cotton fabric used
as a chair
covering.

An example of
18th-century chair-
cover tapestry.

# Not Just Chairs...

A Victorian adjustable piano stool.

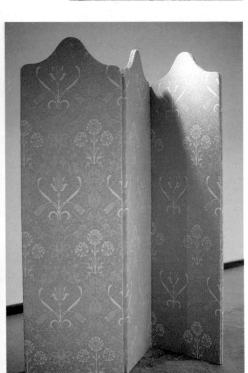

Damask wall covering put up in the
lounge of a private house. Corners and
edges have been braided.

A three-fold screen, covered and ready
for finishing.

# Design

The dimensions and proportions used in seating design are based principally on the provision of comfort for the user. This has to be related to the likely user and the specific uses of different types of chair.

An awareness of the requirements of proportion, shape and the basic dimensions of comfort helps the upholsterer in creating, with suspension and fillings, the necessary depths and angles, particularly in stuffover work.

The outline of a chair frame is generally set by its designer, but the slope of a seat or the angle of a back support or the height of an arm rest will often be governed by the choice and thickness of the materials used; thus the upholsterer is often responsible for the final sitting position and the support experienced by the end user.

When appropriate, the client should be consulted and their requirements taken note of. If there is no particular customer involved, the upholstery work can be based purely on the design and the proportions dictated by the type of frame, its age or period.

## Average dimensions for different types of chair (Fig 3.26)

### Dining and general seating
- Seat height    15⅜–16⅛in (390–410mm)
- Seat depth    16½in (420mm)
- Seat width    15¾in (400mm)
- Slope of seat    3°
- Height of back above seat    16¾in (425mm) (min)
- Overall height    31½in (800mm) (min)
- Angle between back rest and seat    93–95°

### Occasional seating
- Seat height    15–16⅛in (380–410mm)
- Seat depth    16⅞–19¾in (430–500mm)
- Seat width    19¾–20⅞in (500–530mm)
- Slope of seat    4–5°
- Height of back above seat    17¾in (450mm) (min)
- Overall height    27½in (700mm) (min)
- Angle between back rest and seat    105–110°

### Lounge seating
- Seat height    13¾–16½in (350–420mm)
- Seat depth    19¼–19¾in (490–500mm)
- Seat width    19¾–21⅝in (500–550mm)
- Slope of seat    4–5°
- Height of back above seat    22⅝in (575mm) (min)
- Overall height    33⅜in (850mm) (min)
- Angle between back rest and seat    110°
- Height of armrest above seat    6¾in (170mm)

**Fig 3.26 The requirements of proportion, shape and comfort in seating.**

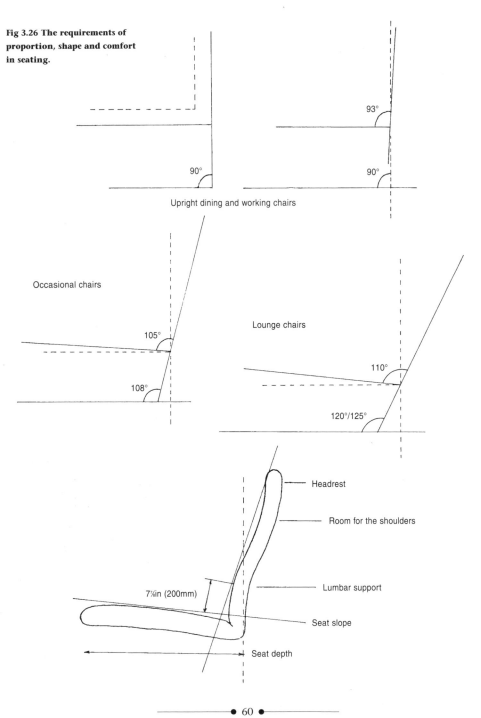

Upright dining and working chairs

93°

90°

90°

Occasional chairs

Lounge chairs

105°

108°

110°

120°/125°

Headrest

Room for the shoulders

Lumbar support

7⅞in (200mm)

Seat slope

Seat depth

# CHAPTER 4

# Interior Upholstery

## Webbings

These are strips of tightly woven fabric, made in different widths, from 2–4in (50–100mm), and they have provided the foundation to upholstery for well over 250 years.

Today, man-made yarns such as rayon, nylon and polypropylene, are blended with natural fibres like flax, jute and cotton, to improve strength and stability and produce strong, durable modern webbings. A good webbing must have a strong selvedge. Cotton and flax have traditionally been used for this purpose.

Different webbings can be recognized by their colour, weave and weight. Traditional types are either pale brown, black and white mixed, or brown and white mixed, and the purely synthetic types are dark brown and black. The quality of a webbing is measured by its weight in pounds per 1 gross yard (metric equivalent: kilograms per 129.6m). The different types are shown below:

- Best flax, pale brown colour, double chevron weave. Weight: 12–15lb. Composition: 100% pure flax.
- English, black and white colour, double chevron weave. Weight: 10lb. Typical compositions: dyed flax and cotton or 79% jute and 21% cotton.
- English, brown and white colour, double chevron weave (twill). Weight: 10lb. Composition: undyed jute, cotton and rayon.
- Common jute, pale brown colour, plain weave. Weight: 9–12lb. Composition: 100% jute.
- Synthetics, brown or black colour, plain weave. Weight: very lightweight. Composition: polypropylene.

**Fig 4.1 Webbings.**

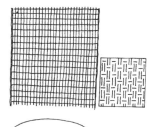

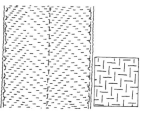

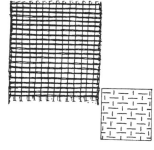

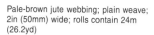

Pale-brown jute webbing; plain weave; 2in (50mm) wide; rolls contain 24m (26.2yd)

English, or black-and-white webbing; mainly jute with cotton selvedge; 2in (50mm) wide; rolls contain 18m (19.7yd)

All-polypropylene webbing; 2in (50mm) wide; produced from synthetic tape, and not spun yarn; lightweight but very strong; easily identified by its smooth, shiny surface

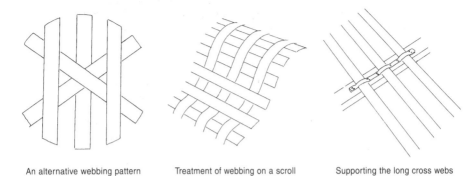

| An alternative webbing pattern for a circular seat. | Treatment of webbing on a scroll end or arm. | Supporting the long cross webs over a centre stretcher rail on a settee. |

**Fig 4.2 Webbing patterns.**

# Lining Cloths and Insulators

## Hessian cloths

Because of their strength and rigidity, hessians are particularly good as lining and support cloths for upholstery. The cloth qualities range from 7–16oz (200–450g) per metre, and those over 12oz (340g) are called tarpaulins. The most popular widths are 36in and 72in (90cm and 180cm), but other widths available are 40in, 48in and 54in (100cm, 120cm and 135cm).

Upholstery hessians are plain-weave constructions with single yarns in both warp and weft directions. When specifying hessians for upholstery, the cloth width is given first, followed by the weight, e.g. 72in, 10oz/sq yd (180cm, 280g/sq m).

As a general rule, the heavier cloths are used for applications over springing and spring units (*see* pages 75–82), because of the obvious demands on their strength. The lower weights are more suited to lining over webbings, outside arms and backs, and for chair bottoms.

- Spring hessian, 12–16oz (340–450g) per metre x 72in (1.8m) wide
- Inner linings, 10oz (280g) per metre x 72in (1.8m) wide
- Outer linings, 7–10oz (200–280g) per metre x 72in (1.8m) wide

Bulk purchases may be by the roll or bolt (Fig 4.3).

## Scrims

Scrim is a fine, plain-woven shaping fabric. Generally, for upholstery work, 8 or 9oz (200 or 230g) jute scrim is used to cover first stuffings in the forming of stitched edges around seats, backs and various shaped facings. Scrim may also be used to build dug rolls and rolled edges.

For traditional work, a good scrim provides the first covering over loose, fibrous fillings, bridled in place with ties or twine, while edge shapes are formed on squabs, cushions, small mattresses, and on fixed chair work. An excellent scrim for traditional work is the 36in, 7oz (91cm, 198.4g) linen upholstery scrim.

## Calico

This is a woven cotton cloth with a fine, plain-weave structure, used as a lining material in upholstery. It is an off-white colour when produced, but can be bought as bleached calico, or dyed black, brown or beige.

The term 'pulled down in calico' refers to a piece of upholstery, lined and upholstered over the second stuffing, but not yet top covered. It is common practice to line good quality upholstery with calico. This allows the calico to take the strain and tension before the cover is applied. The final cover will also give better and longer service when the upholstery is lined.

For upholstery purposes, a medium weight of 5oz per sq yd (140g per sq m) of calico is suitable for most work. Occasionally a heavier weight may be chosen for lining or covering, where, for instance, a loose detachable cover is to be made, or where the calico is to remain as the outer cover.

## Ticking

This is a strong twill-weave fabric, with a slightly stiff feel and a narrow black stripe in the warp direction. It is reasonably proof against fibrous filling materials, such as feathers, hair, flocks and kapok (*see* pages 66–8). Ticking is often used to advantage in upholstery, particularly where feather- and kapok-filled cases are being incorporated into the seats, backs and ends of chairs and couches. Linen tickings are available, or as unions of 50% cotton/50% linen. Hair-filled squabs (cushion pads) are often made up and tufted in ticking.

## Cambric

A fine, strong, all-cotton fabric, plain woven from fine bleached cotton, with a very smooth surface and usually glazed. Cambric is an excellent lining cloth, and for upholstery purposes is down proofed with a waxing process. When making up cambric into cushion cases, the shiny side should be on the inside, to help movement of fillings.

## Platform cloths

Strong, neutral-coloured woven cloths are used for upholstered platforms in chair and settee seats, and inside backs. Platform cloths are also used to cover base upholstery beneath loose or reversible cushions. A platform cloth

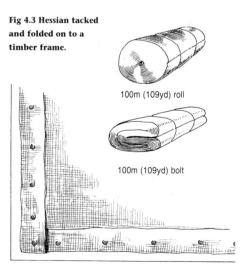

**Fig 4.3 Hessian tacked and folded on to a timber frame.**

100m (109yd) roll

100m (109yd) bolt

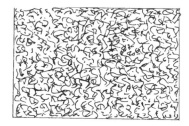

Fibretex non-woven lining cloth

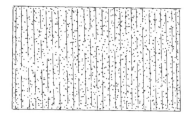

Fibretex non-woven polypropylene

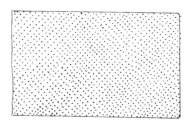

Corovin non-woven underlining

Typar spun-bonded lining cloth

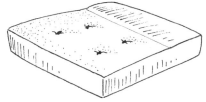

Non-woven cloth used on the underside of a cushion

needs to be visually acceptable as an outer cover, but at the same time, very durable and able to stand up to constant flexing and movement while the chair is being used.

There are several types of cloth which are suitable for the job:

- A heavy-duty bleached and dyed calico, or dyed cotton duck are both plain woven and strong.
- Linen Holland is another plain, flat cloth, reasonably strong and of medium weight.
- Repp is a plain-woven, strong and slightly flexible fabric made from cotton, or a blend of cotton and wool. It has a fine-rib structure running in the warp direction.
- Bedford cord is another warp-rib fabric. It is slightly flexible, has good thickness and the heavy grades may be plain or twill weave. An excellent platform cloth.

## Stockinet

A single jersey fabric, knitted from cotton, rayon or other synthetic yarns. This fabric has tremendous stretch qualities, particularly in the weft direction. It is used as a lightweight lining cloth to contain foam-cushion interiors and synthetic fibre fillings. It holds them in place and makes handling easier.

## Non-woven fabric linings (Fig 4.4)

The non-woven fabrics used in furniture as support cloths and linings are the spun-bonded type. Heavier weights of this type of fabric are used for upholstery in place of traditional hessian, and as underlinings for those areas that require a strong fabric and

**Fig 4.4 Non-woven fabric linings.**

are not normally seen.

The following is a typical specification of cloth weights and densities for upholstery applications:

| | | | | |
|---|---|---|---|---|
| Average weight (g/sq m) | 100 | 125 | 140 | 155 |
| Fibre denier | 5 | 5 | 5 | 5 |
| Breaking strength (N/cm) | 40 | 50 | 70 | 90 |

Colours are white, grey, brown and black
1lb = 4.5N (Newtons)

Properties of these fabrics include good strength for sewing and stapling, and dimensional stability. They are also non-fraying, insect and mildew resistant, odour-free, non-allergic, air permeable, and they have good tear strength. Some particular applications are: insulation over springs; general lining of arms, insides, outsides and bottom; valance linings; base cloths for pad fillings; and underlays.

## Buckram

Glue, size and starch are all used to produce a stiffened fabric called buckram. The material is similar in nature to a heavy cardboard, but with the strength and flexibility of a fabric. Buckram can be cut, folded or shaped, used to support corners, reinforce edges, used for back tacking, and for supporting outsides. Buckram is used in pelmet making for windows.

## Insulating and lining (Fig 4.5)

Suspension systems in upholstery made from rubber products or steel springing require good insulation (*see* pages 75–84). Hessian and non-woven polypropylene

**Fig 4.5 Seat platforms.**

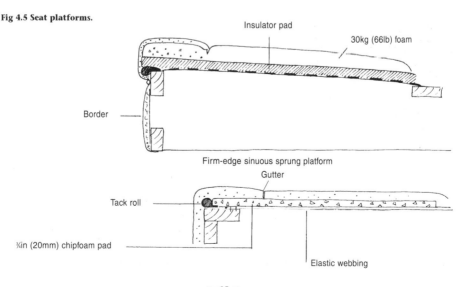

Insulator pad

30kg (66lb) foam

Border

Firm-edge sinuous sprung platform

Gutter

Tack roll

¾in (20mm) chipfoam pad

Elastic webbing

cloths are used as first coverings, followed by pads of good density designed for this purpose.

Lining pads over tension springs or rubber-webbed seats can be made up by taking two pieces of strong, plain, platform cloth and cutting them to the width of the seat, long enough to fix below the back and front seat rails. Machine sew the two pieces along each side, and then turn. To complete the pad, a filling of firm ⅜in (10mm) thick foam or three layers of skinwadding is inserted into the platform cloth bag.

Insulating pads form the basis of upholstery work over all types of suspension. They do the same job as the first stuffings in traditional upholstery, providing a firm but flexible foundation under the softer foams and fillings.

Lining cloths are used to line up chairs and settees on all areas that are not boarded with hardboard or millboard panels. There are a range of hessians or non-woven polypropylene cloths to choose from. Hessians tend to be graded in ounces per square yard, e.g. 7½, 10 and 12oz, and polypropylene in grams per square metre: 75g and 100g. Generally, the heavier the weight per square yard or metre, the tougher and more durable the cloth will be in use.

# Fillings

A good upholstery filling should have high-bulk properties, not be too heavy, and be resilient and strong. The degree of hardness or feel is very important, and it is this quality which makes a filling suitable either as a first or a second stuffing. The stronger, firmer types make good insulators, and the softer, lighter ones make better toppings.

All filling materials are tested and treated to conform with the Furniture and Furnishings (Fire) (Safety) Regulations 1988 (*see* page 00).

## Animal fibre fillings

### Curled hair fillings
The term curled hair is now widely used to describe a mixture of pig hair and cow hair. By nature, animal hair is resilient and durable. Fibre length varies from 1–20in (25–500mm).

Curled hair fillings are marketed to the upholsterer in three different forms, and can be selected for different types of work. Loose hair filling, in three qualities, is bought in 56lb (25kg) bags: hog and cow hair mixture, pure cow tail, and pure horse hair. Hair pads are dense, prefabricated pads about 1in (25mm) thick, 24–72in (60–180cm) wide and any length required.

Rubberized hair sheet is another way in which curled hair is fabricated into easily used sheeting. Three densities are produced: light, medium and heavy, at 1in and 2in (25 and 50mm) thicknesses. Rubberized hair offers the upholsterer a low-cost, flexible, fire-resistant filling, easily shaped and fixed, combining the resilience of a rubber product with the durability and feel of curled animal hair.

### Specifications

- 1in (25mm) sheet, light density, 24oz (670g)
- 1in (25mm) sheet, medium density, 36oz (1000g)
- 2in (50mm) sheet, medium density, 36oz (1000g)
- 1in (25mm) sheet, heavy density, 48oz (1340g)
- Sheet size, all 2m x 1m

## Wool felt or black felt

A soft and resilient top stuffing, made partly or wholly from a variety of woollen fibres. Wool felts are manufactured in the same way as cotton felts, by garnetting and layering to produce 20m (22yd) rolls of three widths: 20in, 24in and 27in (510mm, 610mm and 685mm). Weights are 2½oz (70g) per sq ft and 4oz (115g) per sq ft.

Wool felts are blue-grey with a mixture of many other colours in the form of yarns and reclaimed wools. They have a slightly softer, warmer feel than cotton felt, and by nature have a better tensile strength.

## Flock fillings

Washed flock is a general term for a composition of new and old materials and textiles, shredded and carded into a mass of clean fibre and prepared for use as loose fillings. The wool content will vary from 85 down to 50%, depending on quality. Washed flocks are recognized by their grey-blue colour with some other colours mixed in. In loose form, flocks are sold in 56lb (25kg) sacks, or in smaller amounts by arrangement. This filling is a top stuffing which may be used on its own or over fibre and hair first stuffings.

## Woollen flock

This is a better quality flock filling, containing never less than 70% wool fibres. It is similar in colour to washed flock, but it has much better resilience and bulk with less weight. This filling serves the same purpose in upholstery as ordinary flock filling.

## Feather and down fillings (Fig 4.6)

These are one of the few natural fillings not to have been superseded by modern fillings, due to their relatively low cost, availability and unique feel. Feather and down fillings are available in many different blends and qualities. These include the following: down, which is the covering of young birds and the under-covering of adult birds; eiderdown, the rare and expensive under-coating of the sub-arctic eider duck; goose feathers, a springy and buoyant filling; duck feathers, not quite so valuable as goose feathers; poultry – chicken, turkey etc. – relatively low buoyancy, these should not be used where good resilience is required.

Fig 4.6 Feather and down fillings.

Pure down

Goose feather

Duck feather

Poultry feather

### Blending and specifications

For cushions and quilts, pure down is not suitable as a 100% filling, since curled feathers have much better

**Fig 4.6 (continued)**

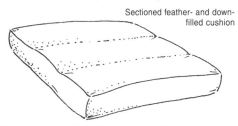

Sectioned feather- and down-
filled cushion

Two-part feather-filled pillow, designed to be fixed
down over a foam base

bulk and resilience. Mixtures and
gradings are given below:

- Pure down – with permissible 35% fine feather
- Feather/down – a minimum of 51% feathers mixed with down
- Down/feathers – a minimum of 51% down mixed with feathers
- Feather – goose, duck or poultry 100% or mixed, as labelled
- Featherdown – stripped feather fibre
- Chopped feathers – usually poultry

## Vegetable fibre fillings
### Coconut (coir) fibre (Fig 4.7)

This is the main vegetable fibre used as an upholstery filling. The raw material for this tough and durable filling is provided by the outer husk of the coconut. Loose coir fibre makes an excellent first stuffing, or scrim stuffing for traditional work. By nature it is coarse, strong and reasonably resilient. It packs and forms well, and can be stitched to a firm strong edge. Coir-fibre pads are prefabricated by layering on to hessian or woven polypropylene. A base cloth of 7oz per yd (218g per m) is used, with a fibre density of 5oz (140g) per sq ft. Pads are 27in and 36in (675mm and 900mm) wide for upholstery purposes.

### Specifications
- Coir fibre, loose, black-dyed, in bags of 55lb (25kg)
- Coir fibre, loose, natural ginger, in bags of 55lb (25kg)
- Curlifil, loose, natural colour, in bags of 55lb (25kg)
- Fibre pads, 5oz (140g) per sq ft, 27in and 36in (675 and 900mm) wide by 20m (22yd) rolls, larger or cut sizes to order

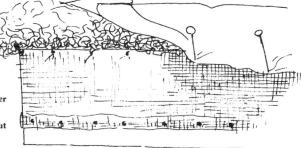

Fig 4.7 Coir fibre first
stuffing tied down over
a spring edge, and a
twisted rope of coconut
fibre.

## Algerian fibre

This is not widely used in the industry, but is still available in loose form as a first stuffing. Made from shredded and dried palm leaves, it is usually dyed black, and is about the same weight and density as coir fibre, though slightly softer. Pre-formed fibre pads are produced by needling on to 7oz (200g) hessian cloth. Algerian fibre does not pack down as densely as coir fibre, has good resilience, and is kinder to the hands of the filler.

## Cotton felt

Cotton felt is a soft, white top stuffing, produced from pure new cotton which is felted and layered into a prefabricated filling, ready for use. Rolls of white cotton felt are 24in and 27in (610mm and 685mm) wide x 20m (22yd) long x approximately 1in (25mm) thick. Two qualities are available, 2½oz (70g) per sq ft and 4oz (115g) per sq ft, the latter being a rather thicker, heavier felt.

The principle use of cotton felt is as a protective layer between fibre or hair and calico coverings. It is used especially in reupholstery, restoration work and all types of bedding production.

## Waddings

Traditionally a cotton filling, which is now only available as skin wadding, with a sprayed surface of cellulose. A 20m (22yd) roll is 18in (450mm) wide and is available in 32oz and 64oz (907g and 1814g) weights. Waddings are folded from a 36in (900mm) width down to 18in (450mm) and can be used single or left double. Wadding is a very useful, smooth, soft, fine padding, which fills a variety of needs in upholstery and soft furnishing.

**Fig 4.8 Uses of polyester filling.**

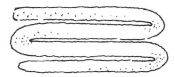

Cut and layered 100% fibre filling

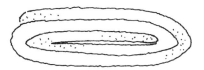

Folded 100% fibre filling

Rolled 100% fibre filling

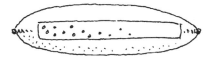

14oz (397g) sewn around a slim foam core

Two pieces of 14oz (397g) sewn around a
slim foam core

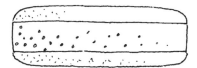

Two pieces of 14oz (397g) batting cut and glued
to a foam core

## Man-made fibre fillings

### Polyester fibre fillings (Fig 4.8)

Polyester fibre is a soft synthetic filament, available in different deniers (thicknesses), and produced as waddings, battings and bonded insulators. It is a very clean, white, versatile fibre filling, which is easily handled, and can be cut, sewn or glued to produce clean, soft lines in modern and traditional work. Polyester fibre is produced basically as a top stuffing, or as a wrap, in many different weights and densities. It blends extremely well with all types of foam and makes a good overlay in the finishing of traditional upholstery.

The two types of fibre are solid and hollow, and these are shaped to give varying degrees of resilience and feel. The fibre is produced in short staple length, or as continuous filament. All these physical characteristics are used to provide a variety of fillings for different uses.

### Specifications

| | | |
|---|---|---|
| ● Wadding | 27in x 2½oz/sq yd | 50m rolls |
| | 27in x 4oz/sq yd | 40m rolls |
| | 36in x 4oz/sq yd | 40m rolls |
| | 27in x 5oz/sq yd | 30m rolls |
| ● Batting | 24in x 9oz/sq yd | 20m rolls |
| | 54in x 14oz/sq yd | 10m rolls |
| ● Insulator pad | 11oz and 14oz through-bonded polyester wadding, in rolls and cut pads | |
| ● Loose carded polyester | Standard quality cushion filling, 14lb bags | |
| | Hollofil fibre cushion filling, 20lb bags | |
| | Long fibre, very soft for quilts | |

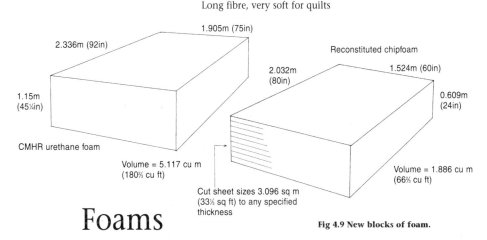

# Foams

**Fig 4.9 New blocks of foam.**

The suitability of a foam will depend on several important factors: how the foam is to be supported or suspended; what kind of job it will be doing when in use; how long the foam is expected to last and go on doing its job.

All foam produced for seating and general upholstery can be specified under the following headings: class, type and grade.

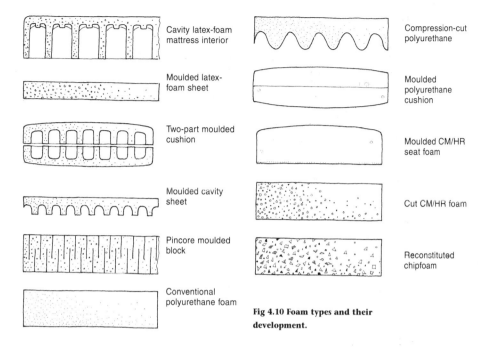

Cavity latex-foam mattress interior

Moulded latex-foam sheet

Two-part moulded cushion

Moulded cavity sheet

Pincore moulded block

Conventional polyurethane foam

Compression-cut polyurethane

Moulded polyurethane cushion

Moulded CM/HR seat foam

Cut CM/HR foam

Reconstituted chipfoam

**Fig 4.10 Foam types and their development.**

## Class of foam

The class of a foam is related to its performance in use, and is determined by rigorous testing of foam samples. The five classes of performance are as follows:

| Class of performance | Type of service | Recommended application |
|---|---|---|
| X | Extremely severe | Heavy duty contract seats<br>Heavy duty public transport seats |
| V | Very severe | Public transport seats<br>Cinema and theatre seats<br>Contract furniture seats |
| S | Severe | Private and commercial vehicle seats<br>Domestic furniture seats<br>Public transport backs and armrests<br>Cinema and theatre backs and armrests<br>Contract furniture backs and armrests<br>Domestic foam mattress cores |
| A | Average | Private vehicle backs and armrests<br>Domestic furniture backs and armrests<br>Component layers for domestic mattresses (excluding cores) |
| L | Light | Padding, scatter cushions, pillows |

## Type of foam

- Combustion modified high resilience
- Combustion modified polyether foam
- Combustion modified reconstituted foam
- Conventional polyether foam
- Flame-retardant-additive conventional polyether foam

All foams are CM/HR types i.e. combustion modified high resilience, to conform with the 1988 Furniture and Furnishings (Fire) (Safety) Regulations and amendments (*see* pages 12–13).

## Grade of foam

The grade of a foam is assessed firstly by its density, and secondly by its hardness or feel. Density is measured in kilograms per cubic metre (kg/cu m), and hardness is measured in newtons (N). Manufacturers give both figures when grading foams. For example:

|        | kg/cu m | N       |
|--------|---------|---------|
| Foam X | 22–25   | 90–120  |
| Foam Y | 30–34   | 115–150 |
| Foam Z | 48–52   | 195–235 |

## Specifying foams

When specifying foams, the type of foam required is decided first. Then the grade is selected, based on the desired hardness and density. Finally, using the recommended application list, the class of foam is chosen. Using Foams X and Y from above as our examples:

Foam X
Type        CM/HR
Grade       22–25kg/cu m  90–120N
Class       A
Application: domestic furniture backs and armrests

Foam Y
Type        CM/HR
Grade       30–34kg/cu m  115–150N
Class       S
Application: domestic furniture seat

### Reconstituted chipfoam

This range of foams is usually specified by density and type only, as their class of use is not comparable with other types of foam. They are all generally in the very heavy and high-density ranges and are also combustion modified.

## Incorrect use of foams

Wrongly specified foams cause general discomfort to the user and a shabby appearance to the upholstery. Performance is the main consideration and therefore class of use has to be correct, but selecting the wrong grade will also cause problems, where a foam is too hard or too soft for its application.

Bottoming is a common fault where a foam does not support well enough and is squashed completely in use, leading to eventual collapse and loss of shape. Bad frame design can also contribute to rails and suspension being felt through the foam.

As a general rule, good performance can be reasonably assured if a minimum density of 28kg/cu m is kept to for all seating applications. Obtaining the right feel will then depend on the thickness of the foam, its grade and the surrounding materials.

## Fabrication

Contact adhesives are applied by scraper, aerosol or spray gun to assemble foam parts. Most polyurethane foams have good stretch properties and good tensile strength, which make shaping and fabrication reasonably easy. Good fabrication relies on clean joints and accurately cut parts.

Some complex foam components are often required to be bent or distorted during fabrication to produce concave or convex shapes (Fig 4.11).

In modern foam work, polyester fibre of different weights is used as a wrapping or topping to finish a fabricated component. This is because a fibre wrap produces a very soft, smooth finish which would be difficult to create with foam alone.

Secondly, the fibre makes a very good protective layer between cover and foam, reducing the possibility of friction and abrasion which can result in fabric wear on the underside. Foam surfaces can be very abrasive, causing pile loss in velvets, and unnecessary wear in most fabrics. Where a fibre wrap is not being used, it is normal practice to cover the fabricated foam in a thin, stockinet sock.

Three-dimensional shapes can be produced by careful cutting and

**Fig 4.11 Working with foam.**

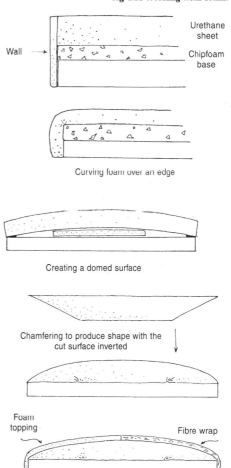

Wall → Urethane sheet

Chipfoam base

Curving foam over an edge

Creating a domed surface

Chamfering to produce shape with the cut surface inverted

Foam topping

Fibre wrap

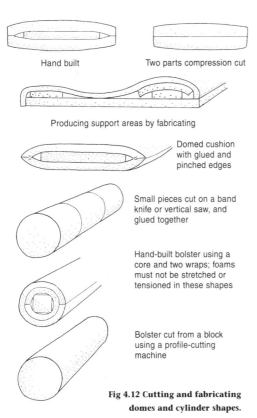

Hand built     Two parts compression cut

Producing support areas by fabricating

Domed cushion with glued and pinched edges

Small pieces cut on a band knife or vertical saw, and glued together

Hand-built bolster using a core and two wraps; foams must not be stretched or tensioned in these shapes

Bolster cut from a block using a profile-cutting machine

**Fig 4.12 Cutting and fabricating domes and cylinder shapes.**

building of foam parts (*see* page 24). Back supports, lumbar supports and headrests are typical applications. Edges can be kept square or made rounded or pinched to a point by gluing (Fig 4.12). Nosed edges (Fig 4.13) can be made by direct cutting on nosing machines, or by hand fabricating.

Chipfoam is quite a firm product, and is therefore often used as a buffer or an insulator for the much softer polyurethane foam; in this way, chipfoam makes an ideal edging and support.

Foam pieces can be drilled and slit to accommodate various features in upholstery. Fly pieces can then be hooked or zipped to form pull-ins through slits in the foam. Buttoning is often more effective and more precise if holes are drilled before covering (*see* page 19).

Where small protruding shapes occur, such as in T-shape cushions, it is more economical to cut the

**Fig 4.13 Nosed and radiused edges.**

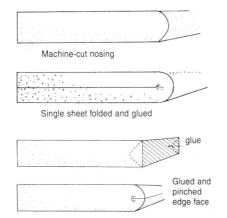

Machine-cut nosing

Single sheet folded and glued

glue

Glued and pinched edge face

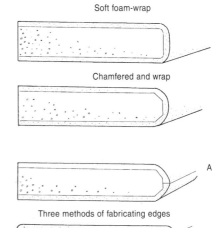

Soft foam-wrap

Chamfered and wrap

A

Three methods of fabricating edges

B

C

main part and add on the shaping pieces by gluing (*see* pages 39–40). Whenever possible, glue joints should be covered by wrapping and not exposed directly to covers.

Foam parts of all types are almost always cut larger by about 5% over the finished size. The increase should be in all directions and ensures good fit in well-tensioned coverings. This extra allowance also takes care of initial height loss which occurs to some degree in all foams when they are first used and compressed. This extra ensures that the corners are well filled and the cover is tight. The addition of a fibre wrap will produce the same effect.

# Suspension Systems

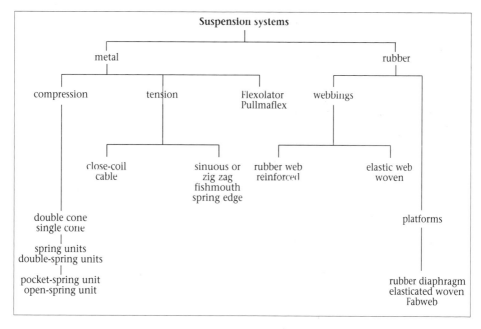

## Springs and springing

Spring steel wire is the basic material for metal spring making. The higher the carbon content in the wire, the stiffer and more resistant it becomes as a spring. Generally, high-carbon wire is used to produced tension springs, while standard spring steel wire is used to make cone-shaped springs and barrel types used in mattress interiors.

Spring steel wire is produced in swg (standard wire gauge) thicknesses, from 7swg down to the very thin 22swg. See page 154 for a table of standard wire gauge sizes.

**Fig 4.14 Spring sizes, gauges and spacing.**

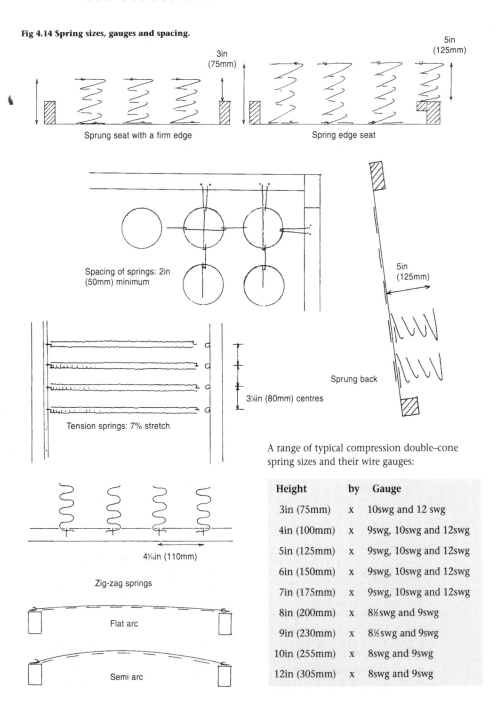

Sprung seat with a firm edge

3in (75mm)

5in (125mm)

Spring edge seat

Spacing of springs: 2in (50mm) minimum

5in (125mm)

Sprung back

Tension springs: 7% stretch

3¼in (80mm) centres

Zig-zag springs

4⅜in (110mm)

Flat arc

Semi arc

A range of typical compression double–cone spring sizes and their wire gauges:

| Height | by | Gauge |
|---|---|---|
| 3in (75mm) | x | 10swg and 12 swg |
| 4in (100mm) | x | 9swg, 10swg and 12swg |
| 5in (125mm) | x | 9swg, 10swg and 12swg |
| 6in (150mm) | x | 9swg, 10swg and 12swg |
| 7in (175mm) | x | 9swg, 10swg and 12swg |
| 8in (200mm) | x | 8½swg and 9swg |
| 9in (230mm) | x | 8½swg and 9swg |
| 10in (255mm) | x | 8swg and 9swg |
| 12in (305mm) | x | 8swg and 9swg |

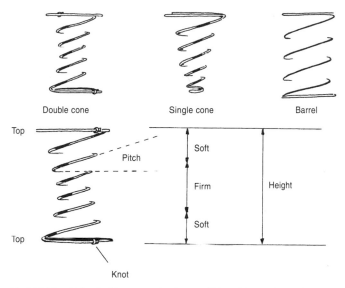

Double cone        Single cone        Barrel

Top

Pitch

Soft

Firm        Height

Soft

Top

Knot

Fig 4.15 (above) The double-cone spring is reversible and knotted at each end. The pitch of each coil is set by the coiling machine and is variable for different springs. As the diameter of the coils becomes narrower, a firm area is produced at the centre of the spring. A single-cone spring is firmest at its base.

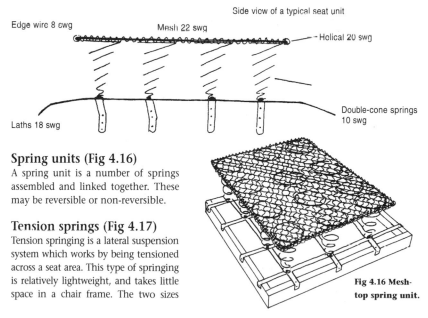

Side view of a typical seat unit

Edge wire 8 swg        Mesh 22 swg

Holical 20 swg

Laths 18 swg

Double-cone springs 10 swg

## Spring units (Fig 4.16)

A spring unit is a number of springs assembled and linked together. These may be reversible or non-reversible.

## Tension springs (Fig 4.17)

Tension springing is a lateral suspension system which works by being tensioned across a seat area. This type of springing is relatively lightweight, and takes little space in a chair frame. The two sizes

Fig 4.16 Mesh-top spring unit.

**Fig 4.17 Close-coil tension springs.**

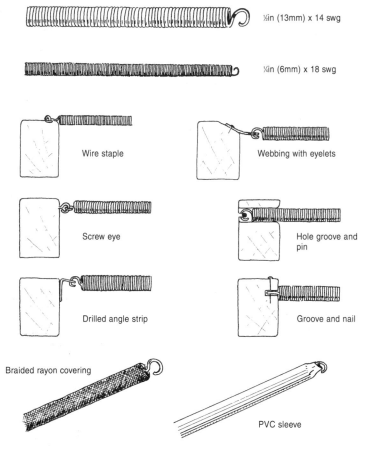

½in (13mm) x 14 swg

¼in (6mm) x 18 swg

Wire staple

Webbing with eyelets

Screw eye

Hole groove and pin

Drilled angle strip

Groove and nail

Braided rayon covering

PVC sleeve

normally produced for upholstery are ½in (13mm) diameter by 14swg, which is used in seats, and ⁹⁄₃₂in (7mm) diameter by 18swg, which is used in back rests. The maximum length for either size is 22in (550mm).

## Serpentine or zig-zag springs (Fig 4.18)

These are tension-type springs, but of a completely different wire formation. High-carbon steel wire is formed into a sinuous strip of various widths and wire gauge sizes. As the serpentine formation is produced, the continuous strips may be arced, semi-arced or flat formed.

The required length of spring should be calculated by fixing a spring at the bottom rail and pulling to the top rail, locating into a clip and adjusting until the suitable curve is found.

Spacing of serpentine springs should fall between 4 and 5in (100–125mm), centre to centre, and clips should be fixed at these centres (Fig 4.19). Link sizes will then be between 2½in and 3⅜in (63–85mm).

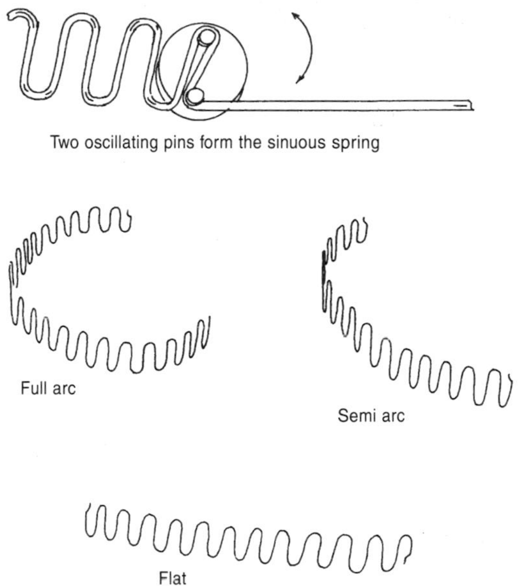
Two oscillating pins form the sinuous spring
Full arc
Semi arc
Flat

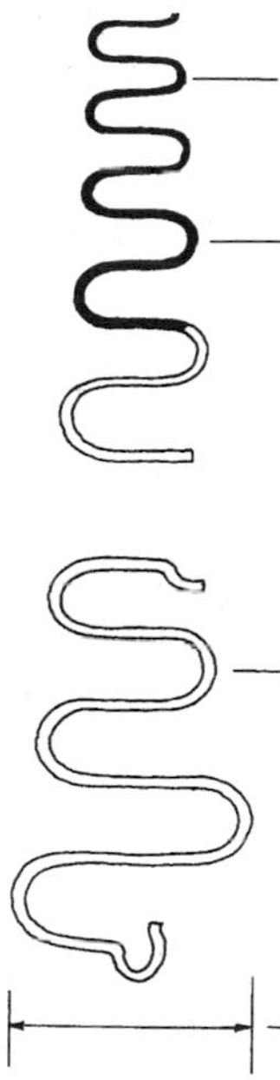
1⅞in
(48mm)
2¼in
(55mm)
2¾in
(70mm)
3in (75mm)

**Fig 4.18 (above) Serpentine or zig-zag springs can be produced in various formations: arcs and end configurations – 1⅞in (48mm) standard zig-zag loop, 2¼in (55mm) medium loop, 3in (76mm) large loop.**

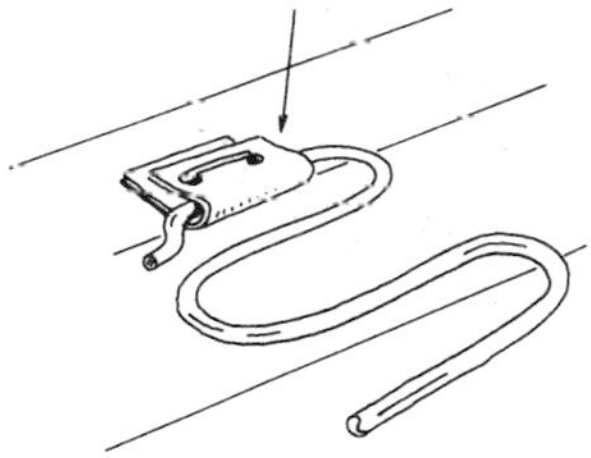
Clip set to inside edge allowing good spring clearance

**Fig 4.19 (right) Serpentine spring clips.**

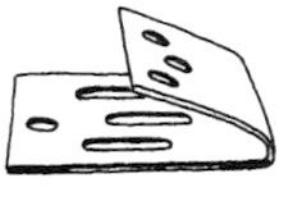
Single-hole fixing with thin-gauge springs

Gauges and sizes for seats:

| Inside seat dimension | Gauge | Height and lengths: 1⅛in (30mm) | 1½in (38mm) | 1¾in (45mm) | 2in (50mm) |
|---|---|---|---|---|---|
| 18in (460mm) | 9½ | 16¾in (425mm) | 17¼in (436mm) | 17⅝in (445mm) | |
| 19in (485mm) | 9 | 17⅞in (452mm) | 18in (460mm) | 18⅜in (470mm) | |
| 20in (510mm) | 9 | 18⅝in (475mm) | 19in (485mm) | 19⅜in (495mm) | 19⅝in (500mm) |
| 21in (535mm) | 9 | 19⅝in (500mm) | 20in (510mm) | 20⅜in (520mm) | 20⅝in (525mm) |
| 22in (560mm) | 9 | 20⅝in (525mm) | 21in (535mm) | 21⅜in (545mm) | 21⅝in (550mm) |
| 23in (585mm) | 8½ | 21⅝in (550mm) | 22in (560mm) | 22⅜in (570mm) | 23⅝in (600mm) |

Gauges and sizes for backs:

| Inside dimension top to bottom | Gauge |
|---|---|
| 16¾ – 1⅝in (425–550mm) | 11½–12 |
| 21⅝ – 3⅝in (550–600mm) | 11–11½ |
| 24⅝ – 7⅝in (625–700mm) | 10½–11 |

**Fig 4.20**
**Fishmouth spring edge.**

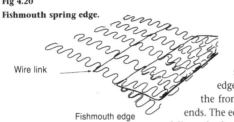

Wire link

Fishmouth edge

## Fishmouth spring edge (Fig 4.20)

A spring edge can be produced for seat fronts by applying and clipping formed strips on to the normal seat lengths. An edge wire is then shaped and clipped on to the front edge of the strips, and returned at the ends. The edge wire is of a heavy gauge and normally follows the frame outline.

## Pullmaflex suspension systems (Fig 4.21)

This is a tension-spring system consisting of a flat grid made up from flexible, tempered wires linked together with heavy-gauge paper-covered wires and paper-centre cords. The grids, which can be of different designs and strengths, are located into timber or metal frames with staples, clips and tension springs. The fixing methods used and the strength of the springs determine the degree of comfort and support of the unit.

Pullmaflex systems are suitable for bed bases, chair seats and backs, and vehicle seating. The system is very lightweight and can quickly be located and fixed into a frame.

**Fig 4.21 Pullmaflex suspension units.**

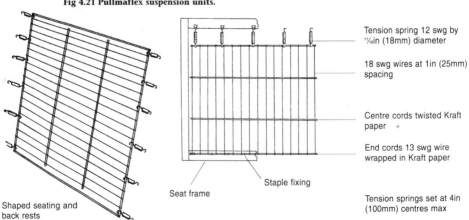

Tension spring 12 swg by ¹¹⁄₁₆in (18mm) diameter

18 swg wires at 1in (25mm) spacing

Centre cords twisted Kraft paper

End cords 13 swg wire wrapped in Kraft paper

Staple fixing

Seat frame

Shaped seating and back rests

Tension springs set at 4in (100mm) centres max

## Selecting springs

Although there are no hard and fast rules on selecting springs for chair work, the following table is offered as a guide:

|         | Gauge (swg) | Height (in)         | Type               |
|---------|-------------|---------------------|--------------------|
| Seats   | 8½          | 8–9 (200–225mm)     | d/cone or hourglass |
|         | 9           | 6–7 (150–175mm)     | ditto              |
|         | 10          | 5–6 (125–150mm)     | ditto              |
| Arms    | 11          | 5 (125mm)           | ditto              |
|         | 12          | 4–5 (100–125mm)     | ditto              |
| Backs   | 12          | 6 (150mm)           | ditto              |
|         | 14          | 5–6 (125–150mm)     | ditto              |
|         | 16          | 4–5 (100–125mm)     | ditto              |

## Spring edges

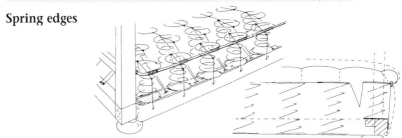

**Fig 4.22 (right) Spring edge.**

**Fig 4.23 (below) Spring-edge profiles and shapes.**

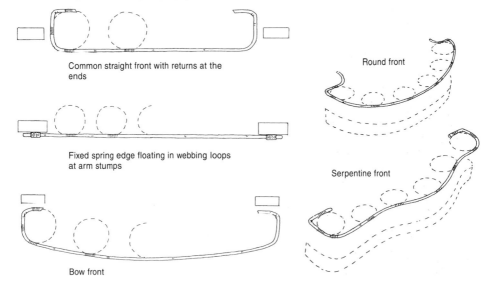

Common straight front with returns at the ends

Fixed spring edge floating in webbing loops at arm stumps

Bow front

Round front

Serpentine front

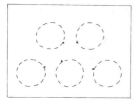
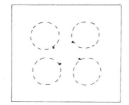
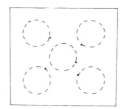

**Fig 4.24 Typical spring arrangements.**

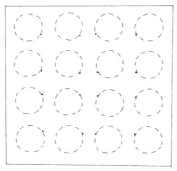

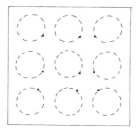

Spring layout for large chair seat

**Fig 4.25 (below) An average layout for a settee seat. An extra row of three may often be placed over the stretcher rail for the longer seat. Two extra springs are added for a chaise-longue end.**

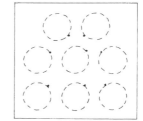

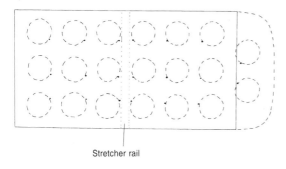

Stretcher rail

Numbers of springs will range from 4–16 in seats with less needed in backs. Spring knots should be kept in the diagonal, with outer edges always clear.

## Rubber and elastic suspension

Rubber suspension works in a similar way to the close-coil tension spring, which it has largely replaced. Using a variety of different fixings, the webbings are stretched and fixed across metal and timber frames, either in one direction only, or interlaced in two directions (Fig 4.26).

The structure is basically a synthetic rubber sheet which is reinforced with synthetic textile cords laminated into the rubber, strengthening the core, and limiting the stretch of the webbing (Fig 4.27). The resulting product is a strong but resilient material capable of supporting heavy weights and producing a feeling of buoyancy associated with comfort.

All types of rubber and elastic webbing can be tacked or stapled to timber rails (Figs 4.28 and 4.29). Care should be taken to see that fixings are adequate and as recommended. Timber rails must be well rounded where webbings are located. Plates, clips and hooks are easily fitted to webbing ends for easier and faster fixings and for application to metal frames (Figs 4.30, 4.31 and 4.32).

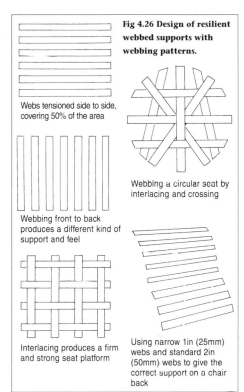

**Fig 4.26 Design of resilient webbed supports with webbing patterns.**

Webs tensioned side to side, covering 50% of the area

Webbing front to back produces a different kind of support and feel

Interlacing produces a firm and strong seat platform

Webbing a circular seat by interlacing and crossing

Using narrow 1in (25mm) webs and standard 2in (50mm) webs to give the correct support on a chair back

---

**Fig 4.27 Rubber and elastic webbings.**

Synthetic textile cords laminated between rubber plies

Stretch

Angled cords limit the stretch and provide reinforcement

Tension

Woven elastic webbing has strong rubber warps combined with polypropylene weft threads

**Fig 4.28 Steel webbing clip.**

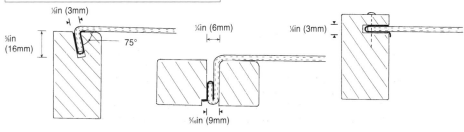

⅛in (3mm)

⅝in (16mm)

75°

¼in (6mm)

⅜in (9mm)

⅛in (3mm)

**Fig 4.29 Steel mortise clip. This allows a neat invisible fixing below the edge of timber rails. The ¾in (19mm) deep mortises can be sloped or angled in the rail to give rake and shape where needed.**

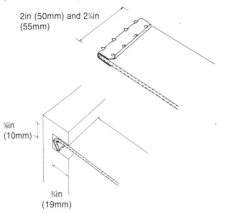

2in (50mm) and 2¼in (55mm)

⅜in (10mm)

¾in (19mm)

**Fig 4.30 (below) Hook fixing into a metal frame. Staple and plate assembly.**

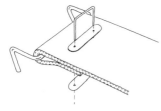

Some typical specifications for laminated rubber and elastic webbings are given below:

## Laminated rubber webbing

Colours: beige, black or brown
Width: 2in (50mm)
Cut lengths or 50m (54.7yd) rolls
Composition: natural and synthetic rubber, with fabric component, multi-filament rayon or nylon and cotton
Thickness: ½in (2mm) approx.
Fabric cord angle: 43°

Woven elastic webbing (Fig 4.27)
Colours: brown, black or white
Width: 1¼in (30mm) and 2in (50mm)
Composition: synthetic rubber warps

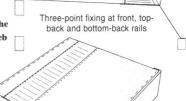

**Fig 4.31 (right) Two versions of the Pirelli Fabweb platform.**

Three-point fixing at front, top-back and bottom-back rails

Two-point fixing with the resilient panel at the rear

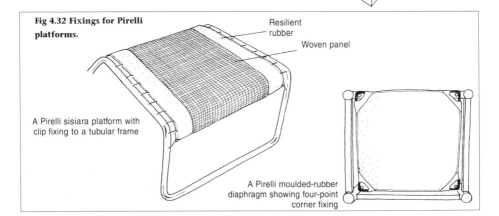

**Fig 4.32 Fixings for Pirelli platforms.**

Resilient rubber

Woven panel

A Pirelli sisiara platform with clip fixing to a tubular frame

A Pirelli moulded-rubber diaphragm showing four-point corner fixing

# Edging

## Dug-roll or tack-roll edging

A large range of edge rolls and trims is available, made from foams, compressed paper and soft plastics. A dug-roll is a simplified version of the edge roll, used to make a relatively shallow edge, or protective lip, on the inside edges of seats, arms and chair backs. Overall sizes vary with each type, but generally fall between ½ and 1in (13–25mm) diameter (Fig 4.33). Some examples follow:

**Fig 4.33 Dug-roll or tack-roll edging.**

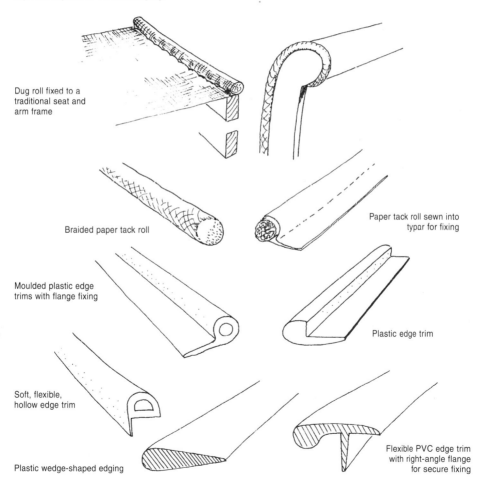

Dug roll fixed to a traditional seat and arm frame

Braided paper tack roll

Paper tack roll sewn into typar for fixing

Moulded plastic edge trims with flange fixing

Plastic edge trim

Soft, flexible, hollow edge trim

Plastic wedge-shaped edging

Flexible PVC edge trim with right-angle flange for secure fixing

**Fig 4.34 Dug rolls or edge rolls.**

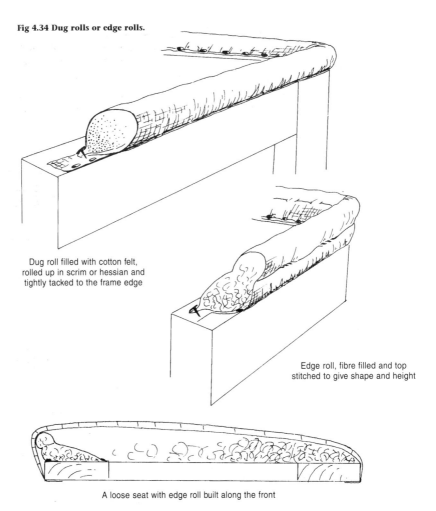

Dug roll filled with cotton felt,
rolled up in scrim or hessian and
tightly tacked to the frame edge

Edge roll, fibre filled and top
stitched to give shape and height

A loose seat with edge roll built along the front

- Profile tack roll, foam, in 100m (109yd) reels
- Typar covered supersoft roll, compressed paper
- Braided paper tack roll, 20mm and 25mm (¾ and 1in)
- Plastic edge trims flat, round and flanged, 9–21mm (⅜–¹³⁄₁₆in).

## Edge trims and rolls

Stuffover chair frames can be trimmed and upholstered with a variety of edge-support materials. Not all edges need such treatment, but those where shape and support are required should be trimmed with a firm edging before fillings are applied. The types used for modern upholstery are similar to the dug roll but are manufactured from compressed paper, plastics or moulded foams. Seat fronts in particular require trims of this type to reduce the sharpness of rails and to give support to foams and fillings. The use of ready-made edgings reduces foam thicknesses and produces a stuffover edge with shape and depth. Other edges best treated with a roll of some kind are arm fronts and inside arm and wing frames.

Where roll-over effects are to be produced, a large edge trim is fixed to overhang the frame. Foams and cover can then be shaped around the trim.

Small edge trims are also used by stapling around outer frame edges so that a lip is formed. The lip is similar to a large piping and produces a convenient edge against which outside coverings can be closed and finished.

An edge roll can be fixed to overhang a seat or arm front. This extends the line of the upholstery and makes a ledge against which a border can be back-tacked or so that a facing can be set in.

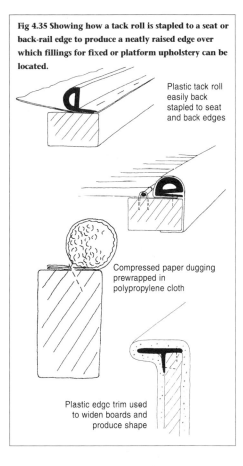

Fig 4.35 Showing how a tack roll is stapled to a seat or back-rail edge to produce a neatly raised edge over which fillings for fixed or platform upholstery can be located.

Plastic tack roll easily back stapled to seat and back edges

Compressed paper dugging prewrapped in polypropylene cloth

Plastic edge trim used to widen boards and produce shape

# Traditional Seat Types

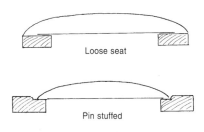

Loose seat

Pin stuffed

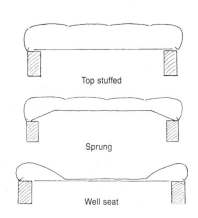

Top stuffed

Sprung

Well seat

Fig 4.36 Examples of a variety of heights and edge shapes to suit different purposes.

# CHAPTER 5

# Machine Sewing

## Machine-sewn Stitches and Seams

### Stitches

The following is a list of those stitch types most commonly used in upholstery sewing. Approximate thread consumption ratios are also given, but 5% should be added for thread wastage.

| Stitch type | | Inches of thread to 1in of seam | Length in mm to 25mm of seam |
|---|---|---|---|
| BS 301 | Lock stitch | 2½ | 63 |
| BS 101 | Single chain stitch | 4 | 100 |
| BS 401 | Two-thread chain stitch | 5½ | 138 |
| BS 304 | Lock-stitch zig-zag | 7 | 175 |
| BS 504 | Overlock, three-thread | 14 | 350 |
| BS 801 | Safety stitch, four-thread | 17½ | 425 |

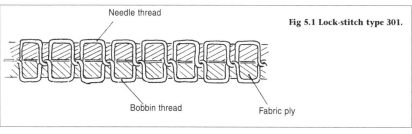

Needle thread

**Fig 5.1 Lock-stitch type 301.**

Bobbin thread

Fabric ply

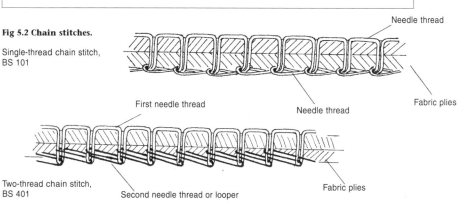

**Fig 5.2 Chain stitches.**

Single-thread chain stitch, BS 101

Needle thread

First needle thread

Needle thread

Fabric plies

Two-thread chain stitch, BS 401

Second needle thread or looper

Fabric plies

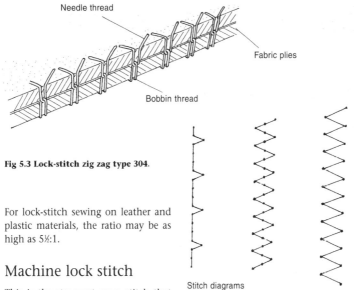

Needle thread

Fabric plies

Bobbin thread

**Fig 5.3 Lock-stitch zig zag type 304.**

Stitch diagrams

For lock-stitch sewing on leather and plastic materials, the ratio may be as high as 5½:1.

## Machine lock stitch

This is the strongest seam stitch that can be produced and uses two threads which lock together at each stitch. The lock-stitch machine uses a needle thread and a bobbin thread, and interlocking takes place in the centre of the joint (*see* page 30). Fine adjustments are necessary to obtain a well-balanced stitch; tension on both threads should be set so that locking takes place inside the plies and not on the surface of either. At the same time the stitch-length control is adjusted to suit a particular fabric or material (*see* page 93). The size of machine needles and the thread being used must be compatible and selected to suit the materials being sewn. Generally, the heavier and thicker the plies, the heavier should be the needle and thread.

## Machine chain stitch

Chain-stitch formation is very different from lock stitch, and tends to be most suited to lighter-weight applications. Chain stitch is not interlocking but is better described as interlooping.

A chain-stitch seam can be produced at very high speeds and works with threads at lower tension. The stitch is formed by a single-needle thread, and does not require a bobbin (*see* page 32). More complex and stronger seams are produced with two- and three-thread stitch formations, all of which are applied by needles and loopers. Although the stitch produced is not as strong or as durable as a lock-stitch seam, it does have some advantages: it allows for fast, continuous sewing, with very little stopping, and for this reason is greatly used in preparation work, e.g. in the making of pipings, zip insertion and other pre-sewing operations. Three- and four-thread chain stitch overlocking machines are used to join and seal fabrics, particularly in loose cover and detachable-cover making.

**Fig 5.4 Seams.**

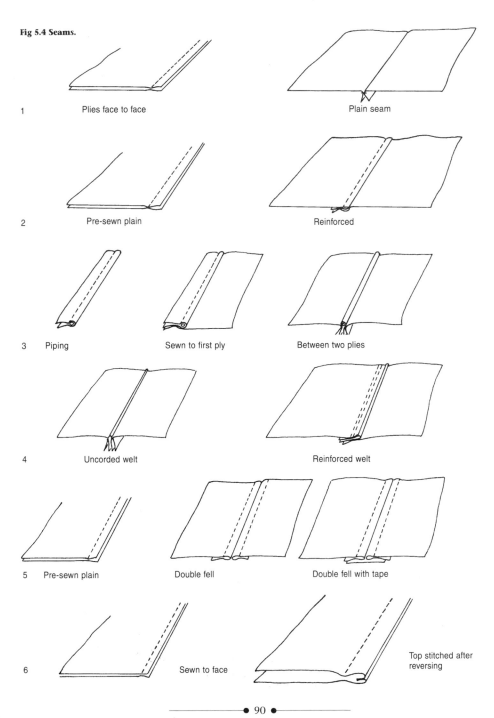

1     Plies face to face              Plain seam

2     Pre-sewn plain               Reinforced

3     Piping        Sewn to first ply        Between two plies

4     Uncorded welt               Reinforced welt

5     Pre-sewn plain       Double fell       Double fell with tape

6            Sewn to face             Top stitched after reversing

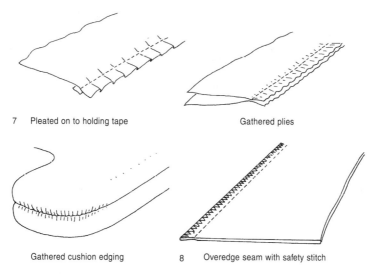

7   Pleated on to holding tape                    Gathered plies

Gathered cushion edging      8    Overedge seam with safety stitch

## Seams (Fig 5.4)

**Plain seam**   Single or double sewn; produces a strong face-to-face joint. Uses: the main jointing method for all covers.

**Reinforced seam**   Plain sewn and then top stitched to produce a very strong seam. Uses: not used a great deal on pile fabrics, but looks best on plain woven flat cloths, coated fabrics and hide.

**Piped or welted seams**   A plain seam with piping inserted between the plies; the piping may be corded or uncorded; produces a strong joint (*see* pages 137–40). Uses: a good general seam which produces a bold and strong joint on most upholstery covers. Used a great deal on conventional loose covers and boxed cushions (*see* pages 118–20).

**Double fell seam**   A plain seam which is top-stitched on a twin-needle machine. This produces a decorative joint. Uses: to decorate and flatten a plain seam on most covers. Looks best on coated fabrics and hides, and flat, plain, woven covers.

**Reinforced fell seam (taped)**   A twin-needled plain seam, with a reinforcing tape laid under. Produces a strong and decorative seam. Uses: mainly where strength is needed on flat areas and around curved, foam-covered edges. Has little decorative effect on pile covers such as velvet, velour and corduroy.

**Top-stitched edge seam**   A plain-sewn edge seam which is over-stitched after reversing. Produces a heavy bold edge. Uses: to support and decorate edges on soft covers and soft hides.

**Gathered seam**   A plain seam which may be taped or untaped. Forms gathering at different densities as a decorative effect, or as a functional seam along edges and around cushions. May be produced by hand or on a machine with a gathering function. It is possible to make all the seams on a lock-stitch and a chain-stitch machine but this is unlikely in practice. Overedge seams, however, can only be made on three- or four-thread overlockers or overedge machines.

**Overedge seam with safety stitch**  A complex four-thread chain formation which oversews the edge of the fabric plies and produces a safety seam parallel alongside the overlocking. Uses: seals raw edges on all soft woven covers and is very flexible. It is ideal on knitted or stretch fabrics. Used a great deal on loose covers, bed covers and washable cushion covers.

# Machine Sewing Leather

Machine needles specially produced for leather work have spear- and chisel-shaped point designs, often referred to as leather points. These are ideal for heavy work on thick hide, and for top stitching and decorative stitching over a variety of seams. Selecting needles is therefore dependent on the type of leather being used, and on the complexity of the seams. The cutting action made by leather point needles tends to produce a large needle hole, and the stitches have a slanting, or zig-zag appearance, better suited to decorative work than standard plain-sewn joints. Thread tension should be checked regularly, especially if hide thicknesses vary.

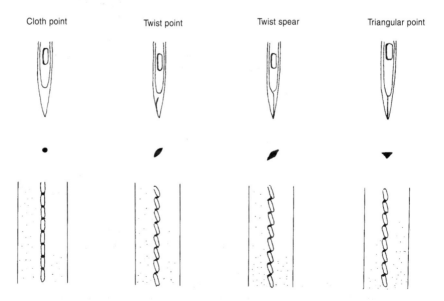

| Cloth point | Twist point | Twist spear | Triangular point |

**Fig 5.5 Seams produced in leather.**

**Fig 5.6 Using leather-point needles.**

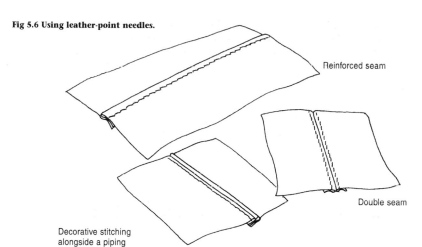

Reinforced seam

Double seam

Decorative stitching
alongside a piping

# Stitch Density

The length of stitch is an important factor to take into account for good upholstery sewing. Stitch length has to be chosen to suit the particular application and the cover type. Generally speaking, the heavier materials should have the lower number of stitches per inch to avoid excessive perforation, while finer fabrics can be sewn with more stitches per length of seam. Stitch length is measured by the number of stitches per inch or per centimetre (Fig 5.7).

Stitch lengths should never be too small for leather work, or seams will be weakened by perforation. Ten stitches per inch (or 2.4mm) is the normal minimum; eight or nine stitches per inch (or 3mm) is a good average setting. On decorative seams, much larger stitch lengths may be used.

# Needles and Threads

Sewing machine threads and needles are chosen by upholsterers according to the weight of material they are working with – generally classified as light, medium or heavy.

Matching a needle and thread ensures that the hole size made by the needle is suitable for the thread passing through it, and a good loop formation is achieved when the stitch is made. If the needle is too small, the thread cannot pass freely through the eye or down the long groove, which may result in fraying and weak seams. Too large a needle produces poor loop formation and causes missed stitches. It is always advisable to keep needle sizes as fine as possible, yet ensuring a free flow of needle thread. This helps to reduce damage to the fabric, and the likelihood of puckering.

## Thread types

As well as the successful matching of needle and thread, a basic requirement for good sewing is the suitability of thread type. Cotton machine threads are made in three types: soft threads are the standard threads with no special treatments. Glacéd threads have a polished surface, giving them extra strength and resistance to abrasion. Mercerized threads have more lustre, and resemble silk. They have good tensile strength.

## Thread sizes

There are two size gradings for sewing machine threads, one for cotton and a separate range for synthetics and blends. In both, the higher the size number, the finer the thread. A range of sizes and their recommended application is given below:

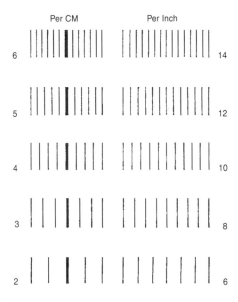

Per CM        Per Inch

**Fig 5.7 Stitch density for upholstery sewing.**

| Choosing the appropriate needle and thread for upholstery sewing | | | |
|---|---|---|---|
| | Lightweight upholstery | Medium upholstery | Heavy upholstery |
| Needle size | 18 Singer 110 Metric | 19 Singer 120 Metric | 21 Singer 130 Metric |
| Thread size | 75 | 50/36 | 36 |

# Machine Sewing Faults

A thorough check on all machinery, carried out weekly or after several hours of continuous use, will greatly reduce many of the problems commonly encountered.

**Condition**   The overall condition of the sewing machine should be good. The machine and its motor should run smoothly and quietly.

**Cleaning**   Cleaning is vital, as lint from fabrics quickly builds up around mechanical parts. Regular cleaning should be done with a nylon lint brush. The rotary hook and the bobbin case are particular areas where regular cleaning is necessary.

**Needles** Ensure that the needle chosen is of the correct class, suitable for both the machine and the work to be done. Check needles regularly for burrs at the point by drawing the finger down and away from the point. A fine burr can be detected this way and corrected using fine emery cloth. When a heavy burr is detected the needle is best replaced. Machine needles are vulnerable to becoming bent. Check a needle for straightness by rolling it along a flat surface, e.g. the machine bed, with the flat of the forefinger. Use the shank of the needle and watch the eye and the point revolve.

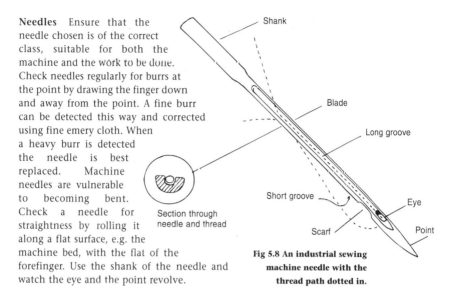

Section through needle and thread

Fig 5.8 An industrial sewing machine needle with the thread path dotted in.

**Hook** The point of the rotating hook or shuttle is known as the pick-up point. This is where the stitch is first formed. The point should always be in good condition.

**Check spring** The check spring is mounted on the upper thread tension control. This should be checked to see that it works efficiently with a positive vertical motion as each stitch is formed.

**Bobbin case** Depending on the machine type, the bobbin case can be removed or checked for its condition and the bobbin thread checked for adequate tension.

**Presser foot** Some sewing problems can often be avoided simply by selecting the correct presser foot: a plain foot for plain sewing, and a piping foot for the making of piping only. Puckering and poor seam quality are often the result of using a piping foot for plain sewing work.

**Threads and threading** Ensure that threads are compatible with the work being done and that the needle used is compatible with the thread. Make sure that the machine is threaded correctly, and check the thread path frequently.

**Lubrication** Remember the oil can. After regular checking and cleaning, all recommended lubrication points should be oiled with a sewing-machine oil. The oil can is the sewing-machine salesman's worst enemy.

**Stitch** Finally, check the balance of the thread tension and adjust to achieve a good stitch formation. The length of a stitch should be set to suit the work being done. Stitch density in upholstery sewing is particularly important.

# CHAPTER 6

# Twines, Cords, Knots and Stitches

## Twines

Flax, jute, hemp and ramie have all traditionally been used to manufacture upholstery twines. They are all strong and durable vegetable fibres, each with its own particular character and properties. Upholstery twines are relatively fine and are graded sizes 1 to 6, size No.1 being the finest. The grade size relates to the number of strands used to make up the twine. Size No.2 is fine but strong and is used for fine stitch work and hand sewing. Size No.3 is a good weight for stitching and the forming of edges. Size No.4 is a heavy twine used principally for tying in springs and for some lightweight lashing work and for buttoning.

When an exceptionally strong twine is needed for tufting, buttoning or lashing down, then a yellow nylon twine can be used. This has excellent resistance to rubbing and abrasion, and so is recommended when movement is likely on a buttoned chair seat or back. Twines are bought in 250g (8.8oz) balls or cops, and there are six balls to a pack. Large 1kg (2.2lb) cops are also available.

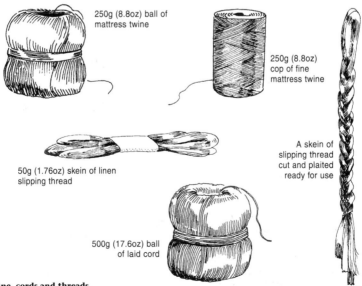

250g (8.8oz) ball of mattress twine

250g (8.8oz) cop of fine mattress twine

50g (1.76oz) skein of linen slipping thread

A skein of slipping thread cut and plaited ready for use

500g (17.6oz) ball of laid cord

**Fig 6.1 Twine, cords and threads.**

## Slipping thread

This is a heavy sewing thread made in several colours; however, the most-used colours are the drab browns which will blend well with most coverings.

Slipping threads, which are made especially for slip stitching and hand finishing, are made from linen (flax) and sold as 50g (1.8oz) skeins, or 500g (17.6oz) cops. These threads are usually wax treated during manufacture. Skeins of thread need to be cut at one end to produce short lengths for sewing, and plaited for ease of handling and storage (Fig 6.1).

# Cords

## Laid cord

This is a heavy lashing cord, used to position and hold any form of springing, both traditional and hand-built modern units (*see* pages 75–82). Laid cord is made from hemp, or flax and some jute, and produced by laying the fibres together with a very small amount of twist, so that very little stretch or give is experienced, and the cord will not slacken after use.

A heavy strong cord of this type has many uses in the upholstery workshop. Laid cord is produced in 600g (21.2oz) balls, with six balls to a pack. 190m (208yd) weighs approximately 1kg (2.2lb). Large 2½kg (5.5lb) cops are made for bulk buying.

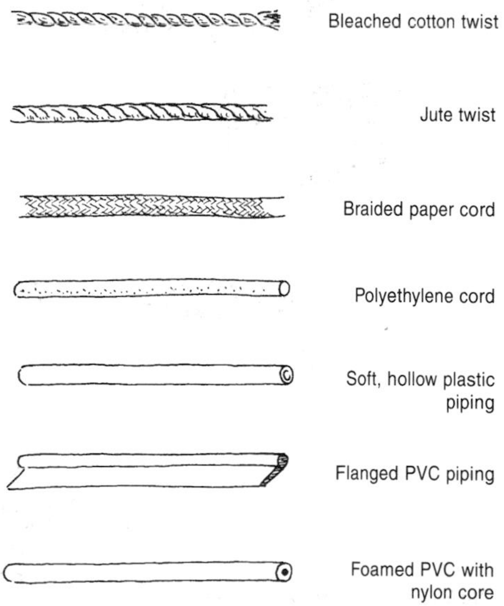

## Cable cord

A lighter weight cord made by twisting two or three plies together, and usually made from blended hemp and flax. It is just as robust as laid cord and will give a little in use; however, it is also reasonably stable and very strong. 320m (350yd) weighs 1kg (2.2lb); balls are 500g (17.6oz) each.

## Piping cords

These cords are made especially for use in upholstery and the sewing trade. The cord may be a filler or core folded inside a fabric strip which is then sewn into a seam or fixed to frame edges. Piping provides a reinforcement, or a decorative edge or an outline in a piece of furniture (*see* pages 137–40). They are available in

**Fig 6.2 Piping cords.**

Bleached cotton twist

Jute twist

Braided paper cord

Polyethylene cord

Soft, hollow plastic piping

Flanged PVC piping

Foamed PVC with nylon core

many different sizes and materials, but generally fall in the three categories of fine, medium and heavy.

Natural cotton twist is the conventional material used for pipings and still remains superior to most others. Cotton is produced as standard or preshrunk pipings and bought in 1kg cops (2.2lb). Some grades and types are given below:

- Cotton twist, natural
- Cotton twist, bleached, preshrunk
- Jute twist, medium only
- Braided washable cord, 4mm and 5mm (⅙ and ⅕in)
- Paper twist, fine only
- Braided paper cord, 4–25mm (⅙–1in)
- Hollow soft plastic cord, 3–8mm (⅛–⅓in)
- Foamed polyethylene, 3–5mm (⅛–⅕in) diameter
- Foamed PVC with nylon core, smooth
- Very soft hollow plastic, 6–12mm (¼–½in)
- Jumbo supersoft, 6–15mm (¼–9⁄16in)
- Flanged piping cords in a range of coloured plastics

For fixed upholstery, the selection of a cord depends on personal choice and cost, but for detachable and washable covers, paper cords should not be used (Fig 6.2).

# Knots

## Slip knot (Fig 6.3)

This knot is one of the most commonly used by the upholsterer, and is used at the beginning of most stitching and tying operations. It is the perfect starting point and not only fixes the twine or thread but also draws together the materials being sewn. In buttoning work, the slip knot is used to fix and draw a button into place and hold it temporarily. As work proceeds the button can then be tightened or loosened on the slip knot as required. A toggle of cloth or webbing is used for the knot to grip and slip on. The depth of buttons for surface buttoning and for deep buttoning needs to be adjustable until the work is even and tight and ready to be finished off. Each knot is finally locked off and secured with the hitch or double hitch (Fig 6.4).

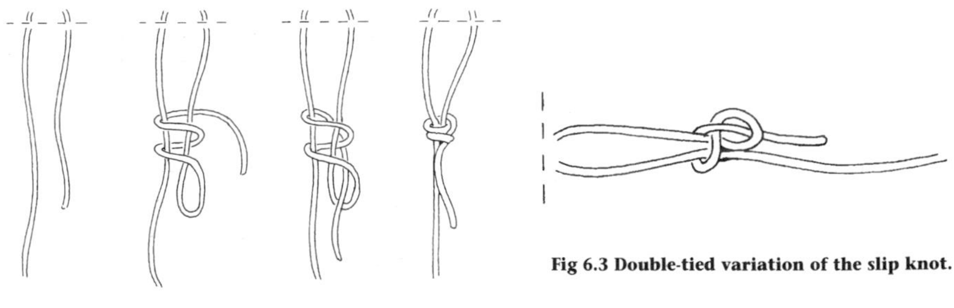

**Fig 6.3 Double-tied variation of the slip knot.**

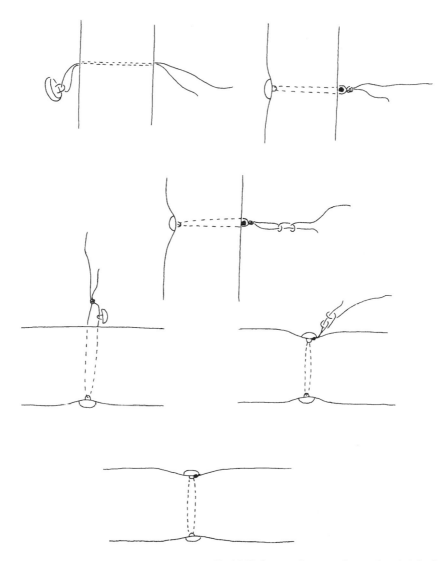

**Fig 6.4 Slip knot used to secure buttons in a chair back and a reversible cushion.**

## Half hitch

The half hitch is used a great deal to lock-stitch a material and to finish off a row of stitching or sewing. Two half hitches together will seal and finish a job before the loose end is trimmed. The slip knot and the half hitch are constantly used to start off and finish most stitching and tying operations (Fig 6.5).

**Fig 6.5 Slip knots and half hitches.**

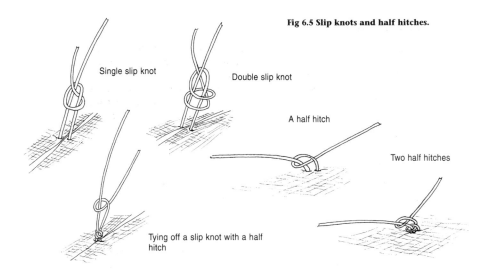

Single slip knot

Double slip knot

A half hitch

Two half hitches

Tying off a slip knot with a half hitch

**Fig 6.6 Tufting.**

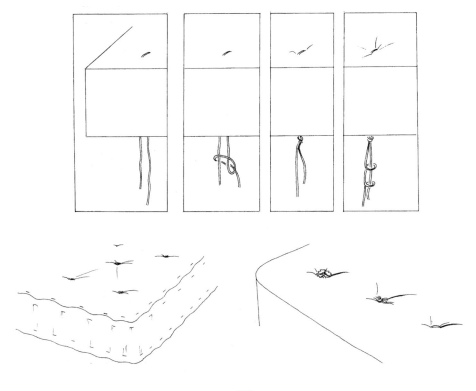

## Tufting (Fig 6.6)

The slip knot and the hitch are used a lot in tufting, which is a technique used to stabilize fillings and set the depth of a cushion, futon or mattress. The tuft is needled through the cover with strong linen thread or twine. A small amount of the cover is caught on the surface, preferably at an angle to the grain of the cover yarns, and the twine is then tied off with a slip knot. Once all the ties are in place they can be pulled evenly to depth, and the work is then turned over for final adjustment and knotting off with a hitch.

## Reef knot and sheet bend

The reef knot (Fig 6.7) and the sheet bend (Fig 6.8) are both easy-to-make knots, used to extend a twine or cord in lashing and stitching.

## Hitches

The various sorts of hitches make interesting and useful knots for fixings and lashings in upholstery. They depend in most cases on the friction created at the point where the cord or twine crosses over. Although a hitch can be made free, it is most effective when tied around something.

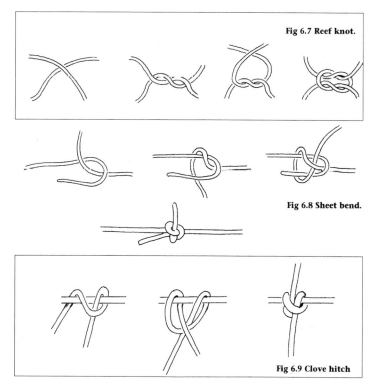

**Fig 6.7 Reef knot.**

**Fig 6.8 Sheet bend.**

**Fig 6.9 Clove hitch**

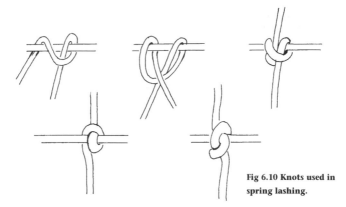

**Fig 6.10 Knots used in spring lashing.**

1   The clove hitch (Fig 6.9) produces a strong and reliable grip on wires and springs. Its reliability makes it perfect for lashing down rows of springs in the seats and backs of chairs.

2   The simple hitch or spring hitch (Fig 6.10) works in a similar way, but is less reliable. It is very much easier and quicker to form, and relies on a laid cord remaining taut. The simple hitch is ideally used alternately with the clove hitch or thumb knot.

3   A thumb knot, otherwise known as the overhand (Fig 6.11), is a relatively simple knot which has a strong grip once tightened. It is ideal for lashing purposes in spring and tying work of all kinds.

4   A simple hitch (Fig 6.12) is basically a loop, and can be effectively used in twin for fixing down and tying off.

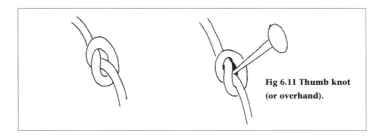

**Fig 6.11 Thumb knot (or overhand).**

**Fig 6.12 Simple hitch used in twin.**

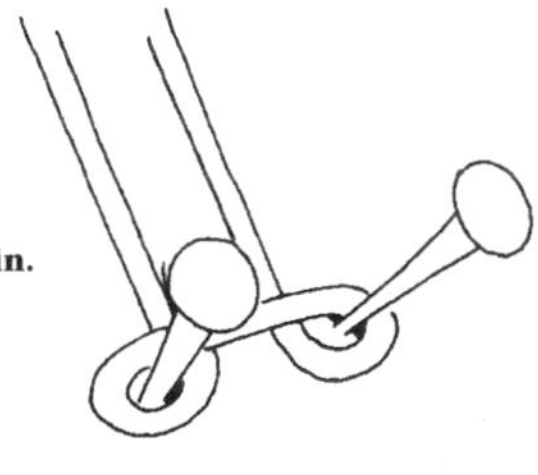

# Stitches

## Lock stitch (Fig 6.13)

This is a strong continuous stitch which locks with a thumb knot as the needle brings two materials together. It is used in scrim work and to join and hold hessians and calicos together.

There are variations of this stitch, but they all do the same job. The spacing of the knots, for example, will depend on the tightness needed and the type of scrim being used. When a good strong join is needed, the scrim should be well caught and knots should be about ½in (13mm) apart.

**Fig 6.13 Lock stitch.**

## Blanket stitch (Fig 6.14)

**Fig 6.14 Blanket stitch.**

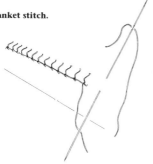

The blanket stitch is easily formed with a straight two-point needle or a curved mattress needle. It is basically an edging stitch and is quite often seen in early Victorian stitch edge work, where a fine feather edge is made around facings and shaped scrolls.

The stitch is spaced approximately ⅜in (10mm) without knots and is simply pulled into place as the scrim and stuffing are squeezed to a tight sharp edge.

## Running stitch (Fig 6.15)

This is used by every upholsterer in all sorts of different ways: a fabric can be gathered on an evenly sewn running stitch; a platform in a chair seat is held in place by a running stitch before being filled, and a pull-in can easily be produced on an inside back or an inside arm by running through the first stuffing with a needle and twine in a neat even running stitch. The twine is eventually covered by a decorative upholstery cord which is slip-stitched along the pull-in.

A running stitch has a knot to start off and to finish with, and so has to be tightened down to depth after the stitch line is in place.

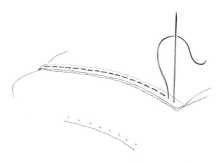

**Fig 6.15 Running stitch.**

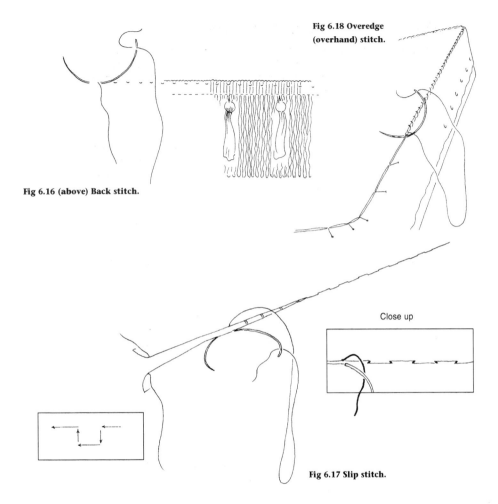

Fig 6.18 Overedge
(overhand) stitch.

Fig 6.16 (above) Back stitch.

Close up

Fig 6.17 Slip stitch.

## Back stitch (Fig 6.16)

The back stitch is one of the strongest hand stitches and is worked from right to left. It can be used as a substitute for machine stitching as the continuous line of stitches resembles a machine-sewn seam. However, for fixing fringes and braids (*see* page 129), the back stitch used in tailoring is extended and spaced so that a very small stitch appears on the surface about every ⅜in (10mm).

## Slip stitch (Fig 6.17)

With care and precision, a slip stitch will be almost invisible when complete. It is universally used to join and finish covers on chairs and cushions and to close up fitted calico linings. The circular slipping needle and a waxed linen thread make a strong durable seam, particularly on shaped and difficult work.

## Overedge (overhand) stitch (Fig 6.18)

This stitch simply oversews together the two folded edges of a border and its main panel. It can be worked very close to form a fine but firm edge, or spaced out to make a softer join. Many bordered edges in 18th-century work were sewn in this way. The stitches were small and close to the edge.

## Whipping stitch

A whipping stitch is similar to the overedge, but has larger slanting stitches. The whipping creates a rolled edge which gives a stiff line when the stitches are drawn up very tight, or when the very tip of the edge is curled over with finger and thumb as the stitch progresses.

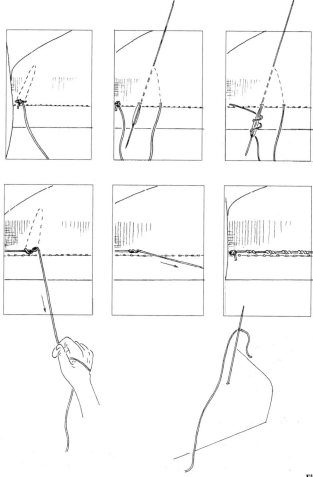

**Fig 6.19 Blind stitch.**

## Blind stitch (Fig 6.19)

This is used to build and firm up the foundation of stitched edge upholstery. It is the first row of stitches put into a first stuffing in traditional work, to pull the stuffing into an edge in preparation for subsequent rows. Its use is common in stuffover seats of all kinds and in panel upholstery with show-wood surrounds. Arm fronts, facings and scrolls are all built using a blind-stitch foundation.

## Top stitch (Fig 6.20)

The upholsterer's top stitch forms a roll edge by compressing and pinching the scrim and stuffing. Depth and tightness will vary with this technique: a very sharp stiff edge would be typical of 18th- and early 19th-century styles, while a softer more rounded roll edge would suit furniture of the late Victorian period.

**Fig 6.20 Top stitch.**

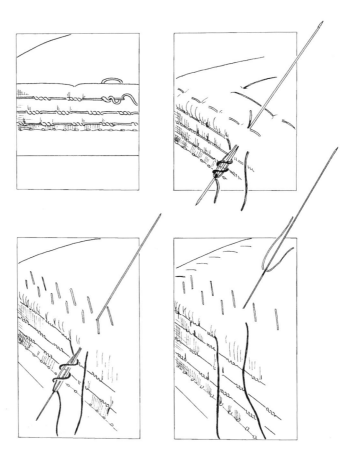

**Fig 6.21 Types of lashing.**

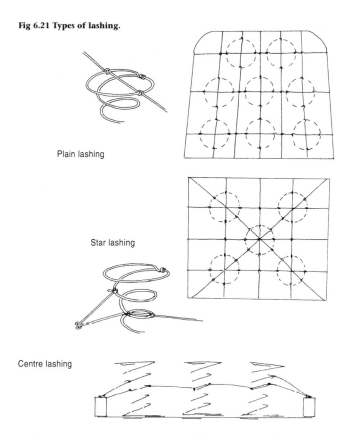

Plain lashing

Star lashing

Centre lashing

The top stitch gives the outline and feel to a piece of upholstery, and will often determine the finish and the way that the covering is treated. Planning ahead and visualizing the finished work will usually dictate the type and shape of a stitched edge foundation.

One, two, or even three rows of top stitch are quite common. These may be worked straight or diagonal; the stitch is basically the same for both.

Two rows of blind stitch and two rows of top stitch will give a good average edge, about 2½in (63mm) high.

## Bridle stitch

As the name implies, bridle stitches are put into traditional work to hold and stabilize stuffing and scrims. Once the bridle stitches are in place, edge building can continue. Temporary tacks or skewers (*see* page 19) can be safely removed, and the bridled scrim will remain square and tightly in place.

Where a seat or back is to have surface shape, then the careful placing of the bridle stitches will help to maintain the shape required. The tightness and depth of the stitches can also be adjusted to produce shape.

# Lashing and Whipping

There is a variety of methods used to lash springs into place (*see* pages 75–82). The springs should be held in compression and not be allowed to move or 'chatter' in use. Plain lashing is produced with two lines of cord, one running front to back and the second running from side to side. A further two rows of cord can be added to form the second method, called star lashing. The extra two rows are put in diagonally, and may run from corner to corner only or may be put in along all the diagonal rows of springs.

Plain lashing and star lashing are applied over the surface of the springs and link the tops of all the springs in two or three directions. A third method is centre lashing, which may be used in addition to the other two, or as an alternative. It is only necessary as an addition when spring heights reach 8in (200mm) or more, and centre lashing stabilizes the group and stops distortion. It can be used as an alternative method on any size of spring and would be chosen when a softer, fairly flat seat is required (Fig 6.21).

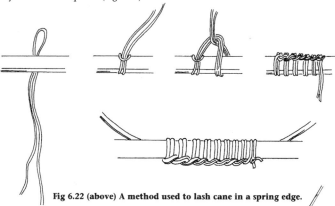

Fig 6.22 (above) A method used to lash cane in a spring edge.

Fig 6.23 (below) Whipping the end of a cord or rope.

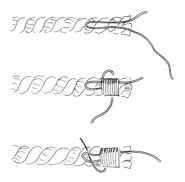

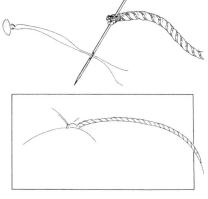

Fig 6.24 (above) Whipping can be used for cording into a button back to form flutes.

# CHAPTER 7

# Fabrics, Coverings and Cushions

## Fabrics and Coverings

An upholstery cover should give good service in the situation for which it is chosen, and at the same time be pleasing and visually effective.

The following is a list of useful qualities to look for in upholstery fabrics:

- Pleasant and comfortable to the touch
- Good shape retention
- Some resilience
- Dimensionally stable
- Good resistance to abrasion
- Good resistance to fraying
- Resistant to fading and colour loss by rubbing
- A carefully balanced composition
- Good tear resistance
- Good seam strength
- Fire resistant to minimum standards

### Types of upholstery cover

Almost all upholstery covers will fall into one of the following eight groups:

| | |
|---|---|
| Woven, plain | repp, tweed, calico |
| Woven, patterned | brocade, damask, tapestry |
| Printed | cretonne, chintz, union |
| Pile | velour, velvet, corduroy |
| Knitted | jersey, laminated, stockinet |
| Coated fabric | PVC-coated materials (vinyls) |
| Non-woven | spun-bonded, stitch-bonded |
| Animal skins | hide, suede |

Apart from hides and various animal skins, upholstery covers are made in piece lengths. These lengths range from 35–100m (38–109yd) depending on the type of cloth, but generally the heavier cloths are the shorter pieces, and the lighter cloths can be made longer.

The majority of covers used for upholstery are piece goods of a standard width. The average width of a cover is 120–135cm (47¼–53⅛in). The length (or linear) measurement is termed 'along the roll'. 'Weft' refers to cross yarns and 'warp' to lengthwise yarns. The selvedge is a tightly woven edge strip and the bias is a diagonal cut or line. The half width is used for estimating purposes (see pages 156–8).

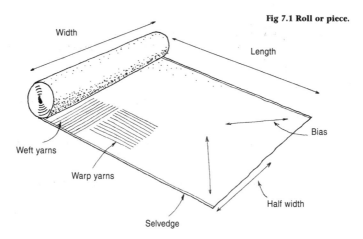

**Fig 7.1 Roll or piece.**

## Textile fibres

The following is a family tree of textile fibres, classifying them according to whether they are natural, man-made or synthetic:

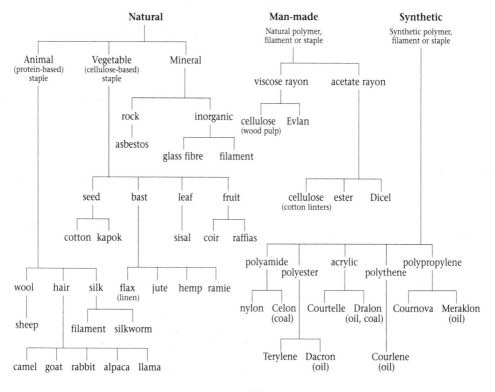

# Structure and type

The following is a list of some of the most common upholstery fabrics, grouped according to structure.

## Plain Weaves

**Chintz**   A fine, close-weave fabric, 100% cotton; plain or patterned and glazed or semi-glazed.

**Cretonne**   A strong, close-weave cotton or rayon fabric, usually with printed patterns; heavier than chintz and sometimes twill woven.

**Duck**   A heavy cotton or linen canvas with natural or plain-dyed colours.

**Repp**   A plain wool or cotton fabric with a pronounced weft rib effect; strong and of good weight.

**Shantung**   This can be made in furnishing weight from silk or cotton with a rough-textured surface. Its natural colour is brown when made from rough silk.

**Tweed**   Blends of wool cotton and rayon are used for furnishing tweeds which are finished with a smooth surface; hard-wearing, pliable and warm.

**Unions**   This is made from a combination of two main natural fibres such as cotton and linen, although today synthetics may be added; strong and durable and will wash easily; usually printed.

## Twill Weaves

**Denim**   A tough, close-weave fabric, produced in plain colours and made from 100% cotton.

**Tartan**   Check designs woven for furnishings from wool and blends of man-made fibres.

**Ticking**   A good upholstery and cushion fabric with a stiff feel; may be cotton or linen; woven stripes are typical, either in black and white or colours.

**Tweed**   A strong woollen fabric with diagonal and herring-bone weave patterns; the simple and coarse weaves make a resilient medium-weight cloth.

**Unions**   Printed and plain-colour cloths with strong, close-twill weaves; a good upholstery and loose cover material.

## Jacquard Weaves

**Damask**   The combination of weaves defines the pattern, which may be one or two colours. Wool, cotton, silk and synthetics are also combined to give matt and lustre effects. Generally the weft forms the background with a sateen-weave pattern.

**Brocade**   A colourful, richly patterned fabric traditionally made from silk with embroidery effects. It is made in a variety of yarns today with the colours running in a stripe formation in the back of the fabric.

**Brocatelle** A heavy and durable upholstery fabric with a raised or padded pattern surface. It is made from strong mercerized cotton combined with silk or rayon; jute may also be added for stability and weight.

**Tapestry** Developed from needlework tapestries and woven on the jacquard loom with pictorial designs and motifs. The structures can be complex and heavy from cotton, worsted and rayon yarns.

**Matelassé** A traditional upholstery cloth construction with a raised surface texture. Cotton and viscose rayon are the typical fibre composition, making a hard-wearing and stable fabric.

## Pile fabrics

**Velour** A smooth short pile fabric made from mercerized cotton with weft yarns forming the pile surface. This is a serviceable upholstery covering with a distinct look of luxury, and shaded effects created by the brush of the fine pile.

**Velvet** A warp pile fabric generally heavier than a velour and made with a variety of different pile yarns. Silk, linen, mohair and Dralon are all widely used to produce a good hard-wearing upholstery cover. Velvets may be plain, figured or embossed and sometimes printed. Genoa and Utrecht are two types.

**Corduroy** Cords run through the length of this fabric and may be fine or heavy. It is made from 100% cotton with a plain- or twill-weave foundation. It is a strong covering with a distinct nap or lay of pile. Corduroy is normally chosen for traditional upholstery work.

**Plush** A heavy, long-pile upholstery fabric which may have a pile of wool, mohair, cotton or synthetics. The pile is often coarse and is not laid. It is durable and easy to clean.

**Moquette** The pile of moquette may be looped, cut, or a combination of the two. Warp yarns form the pile which can be wool, rayon or synthetics, making a very hard-wearing upholstery fabric used today mainly for commercial interiors.

**Chenille** A medium to heavy-weight fabric made with a special weft yarn prewoven to produce a thick pile yarn. A heavily textured fabric, chenille is often made from wool and cotton for furnishing use. Not a true pile fabric but similar in texture and feel.

## Knitted Fabrics

**Warp knits** Two-bar knit fabrics are produced for furnishing purposes and can be laminated to make stable cloths with good stretch. Raised-loop velours are produced on this knitting system, as are Raschel velvets; these make good upholstery cloths and have an extra pile yarn knitted in and cut as knitting progresses. Base cloths for vinyl-coated fabrics are mainly knitted construction.

### Coated Fabrics
**Vinyls and expanded vinyls**   Embossed grain, printed pattern and matt effects are all used to produce attractive vinyl cloths which are robust and very resilient upholstery materials. An expanded vinyl may be up to $\frac{1}{16}$in (1.5mm) thick with good surface resilience and wear properties. They are generally practical, washable and clean looking, for use on contract and public service furniture. Vinyl and expanded vinyl coatings have knitted or woven base cloths.

# Hides and Leathers

The skins used for upholstery leather are specially selected for size and are as free from natural blemishes as possible. They are manufactured to British standard BS 6608, and are fire retardant to BS 5852 Part 1. They are generally through-dyed for maximum scuff resistance and have enamelled or lacquered surfaces for maximum light fastness and abrasion resistance.

Special matching and colourings are always available from the leather companies. Natural aniline-dyed leather and suede are luxury materials which must be treated with care, and not used in conditions where excessive dirt or grease may result in permanent staining. Suede should not be subjected to direct sunlight.

## Types of leather
### Cow hide
This is by far the most popular leather covering for upholstery purposes, and is used for both contract and domestic furniture. Cow skins are large and have an average thickness of $\frac{1}{16}$–$\frac{1}{13}$in (1½–2mm). It is a tough, warm and flexible covering, produced in a range of both traditional and modern colours.

### Suede
The reverse or flesh side of a hide has all the good properties of a leather with the addition of a soft, smoothly shaved surface. Available in a variety of colours and tones, suede is sometimes laminated to produce heavier and more stable coverings.

Oxhide and pigskin are also used as upholstery coverings.

## Properties of leather
- Good tensile strength
- Good resistance to tearing, due to its interlaced fibre structure
- Resistance to puncture
- Good strength-for-weight ratio
- Good resistance to fatigue by flexing
- Can be made dimensionally stable, or very flexible, to suit different purposes
- Has good heat insulation
- Excellent permeability to water vapours
- Absorbs and disperses water well

- Warm in winter and cool in summer
- Good resistance to water and can be made waterproof
- Good resistance to fire, and does not support flame easily
- Mouldability is good, which helps in the upholstery work
- Good resistance to rot or fungal attack

## Shape and dimensions

The shape and dimensions of a typical hide are illustrated in Fig 7.2. This gives a guide to the larger panel sizes that are obtainable. Half hides would be cut from A to B, and the range of dimensions should be calculated at between 40 sq ft (3.7 sq m) and 55 sq ft (5 sq m) per hide. An average size would be 47 sq ft (4.3 sq m). Approximate measurements of the average hide would be:

A to B – 7ft 6in (228cm)
c to d – 4ft 3in (129cm)
e to f – 5ft 9in (175cm)
g to h – 6ft 3in (190cm)
i to j – 6ft 9in (205cm)
k to l – 5ft 6in (168cm)

**Fig 7.2 A full-size upholstery cow hide measuring approximately 48 sq ft (4.4592 sq m). A half hide is cut from A to B.**

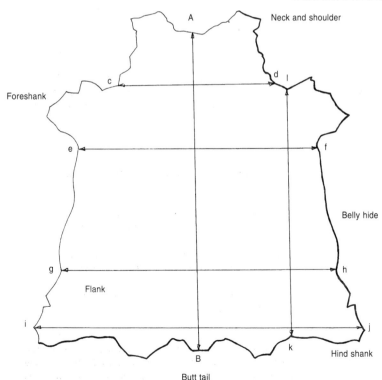

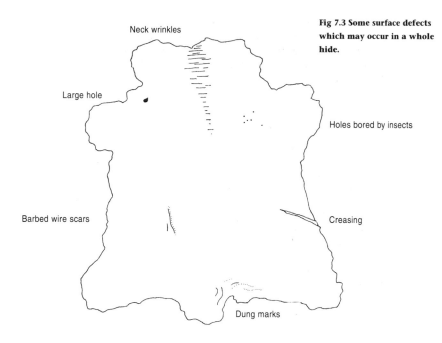

Neck wrinkles

**Fig 7.3 Some surface defects which may occur in a whole hide.**

Large hole

Holes bored by insects

Barbed wire scars

Creasing

Dung marks

Approximately 11 to 13 dining chair loose seats can be cut from one hide of the average size shown; or seven stuffover dining chair seats and one average-size easy chair would use about one and a half hides. 1m of woven soft cover 120cm wide is equal to just over 12 sq ft (1.1 sq m) of hide.

## What to expect and what to check

Before marking out and cutting a piece of hide, it is vital to give it a careful inspection. The following is a useful checklist:

1. Is the colour and type the one that was ordered, and as per sample?
2. Check the area of the hide. Is this exactly the right amount needed or is there some to spare? This will affect the marking out.
3. Check for any natural or processing defects in the surface of the skin (Fig 7.3). When any faults are located they should be lightly marked with a chalk ring around them.
4. At the same time, check the depth of wrinkling along the backbone, particularly along the neck end.

It can now be decided which of the defects must be completely avoided, and which are acceptable for use on some of the less important cuts, e.g. outside arms, outside backs or hidden parts. With a clear picture of the skin in front of you, the larger parts can be marked out, bearing in mind that the many smaller parts will have to be fitted in around these.

## Measuring for hide

To calculate the amount of hide needed for a particular job, first measure the job in linear metres. The area per metre is found by multiplying the required width – say 1.32m (52in) – by 1m, giving an area of 1.32 sq m. For buying purposes this is then converted to square feet by multiplying by 10.7639 (the number of square feet in a square metre) and adding 25% waste to give a total of 17.76 sq ft, which can be rounded up to 18ft.

The same estimated area can be arrived at by using imperial measurements: a fabric width of 52in is multiplied by the length of 39½in to give 14.263 sq ft, which is increased by 25% for waste, giving a total of just under 18 sq ft.

### Example

A chair requiring 4.5m of 129cm-wide cover (14¾ft of 51in-wide cover) will need a nominal figure of 7.5 sq m (80 sq ft).

| | | |
|---|---|---|
| 4.5m x 1.29m | = | 5.80 sq m |
| plus 25% waste | = | 1.45 sq m |
| Total | = | 7.26 sq m |
| Rounded up to 7.5 sq m | | |

Or:

| | | |
|---|---|---|
| 14¾ft x 4¼ft | = | 62 3/4 sq ft |
| plus 25% waste | = | 15¾ sq ft |
| Total | = | 78¼ sq ft |
| Rounded up to 80 sq ft | | |

Nominal figures are used in the workshop to make calculating and estimating less complicated. These are mostly rounded up for convenience to the nearest half or whole figure.

## Tanning

Tanning is a process which preserves and textures the hide and gives it the characteristic odour of fresh leather.

The tanning process involves either mineral or vegetable materials, or else a combination of both. The mineral-tanning substances are chromium salts, which soften the hide and colour it pale blue in a process known as chrome tanning.

The main vegetable-tanning materials are:

- Mimosa – the bark of the South and East African wattle tree
- Valonia – the acorn of a Turkish oak tree
- Sumac – the ground bark of the sumac tree
- Quebracho – wood from the quebracho tree
- Myrobalan – an Indian nut

## Some standard leather finishes

**Chrome re-tan**   Light chrome tanning, then completing with vegetable tans, to give very flexible leather.

**Chrome re-tanned, antique rub-off finish**  Combination-tanned leathers finished with a rub-off finish used with wash-off liquids and sealer.

**Chrome re-tanned – printed grain**  Combination-tanned upholstery leather given an improved artificial grain.

**Full chrome tanned – natural russet**  Leather which has received the full mineral tan, but was left at the russet stage, and coloured pale cream on the grain side only.

**Full chrome tanned, aniline**  A soft supple, chrome-tanned leather which has been aniline dyed through.

**Full-grain hide**  A leather which has not been grain corrected, but retains its natural grain intact.

## Maintenance

Grain leather should be cleaned with a light, circular motion, using a mild toilet soap and a damp cloth. This should then be repeated using clean water only, taking great care not to soak the leather. After cleaning, a leather conditioner should be used, but only those recommended by the manufacturers.

This method of cleaning is all that should be needed under normal conditions, about once a year or every two years.

Discoloration does not affect the wearing properties of leather. Various hide foods, which are recommended by leather manufacturers, are designed to restore the original surface and the feel of leather after gentle cleaning. Wax polishes, spray polishes and saddle soaps are not recommended for use on upholstery leathers.

# Cushions

Cushions for upholstery generally fall into two categories: the unbordered pillow types, and the bordered or box constructions.

## Unbordered cushions

These are simply made up by sewing two identical pieces of cover together. An opening is left along one side for filling and this is later closed by hand slipping, zip or machine sewing. The edges or seams may be trimmed during making up with piping or ruche. Alternatively, cording, gimp or fringe can be hand sewn on after the cushion is made. The outline and shape of an unbordered cushion is partly determined by the cutting plan and partly by the amount of filling used.

Flat squabs or pads are normally hair filled with wraps of cotton wadding, or cotton felt as outer fillings. Cushions of this type are often lined with calico, particularly if the cover is removable for cleaning.

The three most commonly used trimmings are upholstery gimp, silk cords and various fringes (*see* pages 128–9). These can all be applied by hand sewing both on the surface of the covers or along the edges (Fig 7.5).

Envelope and overlay styles can be created by trimming and boxing the cushion corners. This technique is used to remove the pointed corners of the cushion and produce an envelope or boxed corner.

## Boxed cushions

The cover parts required for this cushion are a top piece, a bottom panel and border strips with joins at each corner or, alternatively, along each side.

The choice of seams and trimmings is the same as for unbordered cushions, with some being applied during making up or sewn on after. The making up

**Fig 7.4 Cushion designs and constructions.**

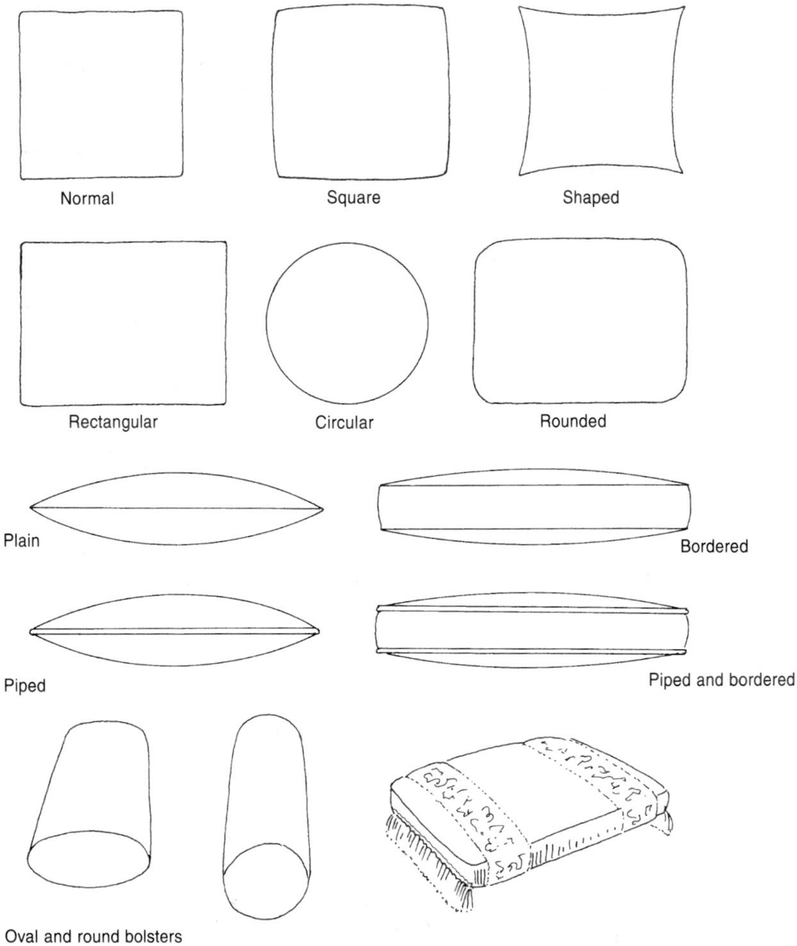

Normal    Square    Shaped

Rectangular    Circular    Rounded

Plain    Bordered

Piped    Piped and bordered

Oval and round bolsters

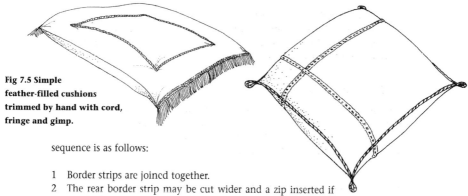

**Fig 7.5 Simple feather-filled cushions trimmed by hand with cord, fringe and gimp.**

sequence is as follows:

1 Border strips are joined together.
2 The rear border strip may be cut wider and a zip inserted if required.
3 The rear border strip is joined to the other borders.
4 The continuous border is then sewn around the top panel and closed off.
5 If the borders are not corner joined, notching is needed to locate the bottom panel accurately.
6 The bottom panel is sewn in, and, where required, an opening left for filling at the rear end.

**Fig 7.6 Bolster cushions.**

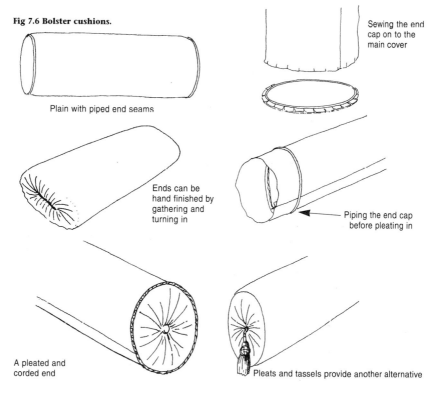

Plain with piped end seams

Sewing the end cap on to the main cover

Ends can be hand finished by gathering and turning in

Piping the end cap before pleating in

A pleated and corded end

Pleats and tassels provide another alternative

Where seams are to be piped or ruched, this is done by sewing these to the top and bottom panels before the above sequence begins.

Pipings, particularly in cushion making, should be bias cut as this allows for some flexibility in the joint and works well around curves (*see* pages 137–40).

## Bolster cushions

Bolsters are usually circular or oval in section and their construction is basically a single curved panel, hand or machine sewn to the end caps. The ends can be varied to produce a variety of different effects (Fig 7.6). The main panel should be notched at intervals along its edge to ensure that the two ends are in line and twisting does not occur, particularly when oval sections are being made.

## Cushion interiors (Fig 7.7)

Traditional cushion interiors can be made up with any of the following filling materials: carded cotton or wool felts, curled hair mixtures, or feathers and down. Each of these alternatives will produce a different feel and they have to be selected and used to suit the type or period of the work.

Allowances chart for cushion covers and interiors

**Cover**

| | example | | |
|---|---|---|---|
| Pattern size or measurements | 20in x 20in (500mm x 500mm) | | |
| Cover thickness (heavy) | deduct | ⅛in (3mm) | all round |
| Sewing allowance | add on | ⅜in (10mm) | all round |
| Pipings, ruche etc. | deduct | ¼in (6mm) | all round |
| Multiples of two or more with space between | deduct | ⅛in (3mm) | overall |

**Interior**

| | example | | |
|---|---|---|---|
| Pattern size or measurements | 20in x 20in (500mm x 500mm) | | |
| Foam and stockinet, 5% | add on | 1in (25mm) | overall |
| Foam and polyester wadding wrap, 3% | add on | ⁹⁄₁₆in (15mm) | overall |
| Feather, 10% | add on | 2in (50mm) | overall |
| Feather and down, 10% | add on | 2in (50mm) | overall |
| Loose polyester fibre, 7½% | add on | 1½in (38mm) | overall |

# Fabric Care

## Fabric testing

Most fabrics and covers recommended for upholstery use undergo several tests to determine their suitability. The results of such tests provide a guideline to those who sell and use fabrics for furnishing purposes. This includes furniture manufacturers, furniture retailers, interior designers and upholsterers.

**Fig 7.7 Modern cushion interiors.**

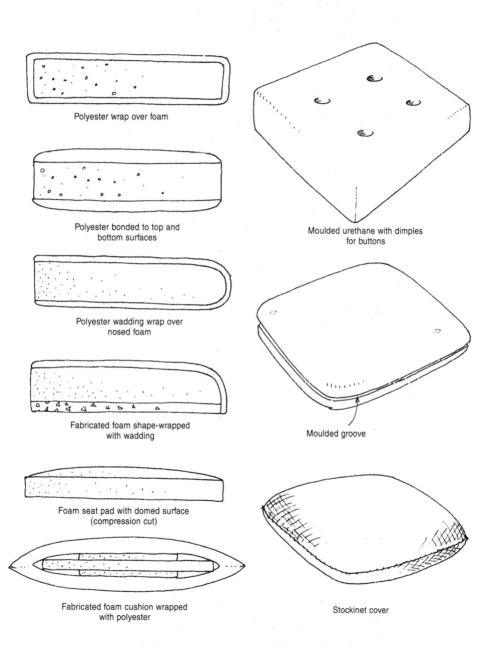

Polyester wrap over foam

Polyester bonded to top and
bottom surfaces

Polyester wadding wrap over
nosed foam

Fabricated foam shape-wrapped
with wadding

Foam seat pad with domed surface
(compression cut)

Fabricated foam cushion wrapped
with polyester

Moulded urethane with dimples
for buttons

Moulded groove

Stockinet cover

### Rub test or Martindale test

This tests a fabric for its resistance to abrasion. Some typical results are:

- 25,000 rubs – poor
- 50,000 rubs – average
- 80,000 rubs – excellent

### Fade test

This tests a fabric for its resistance to fading by sunlight, by wetting and by rubbing. Resistance to sunlight is assessed on the Grey Scale. This scale is set by the British Dyers Association (BDA). On a scale of 1 to 8, each figure on the scale is approximately twice as fast to light as the figure preceding it.

### Tear test

This tests a fabric for its resistance to tearing. A pull-test machine is used (e.g. an Instron tensile tester) to stretch a sample of fabric which has two parallel scissor cuts running approximately half way into the fabric at intervals of a third. The machine measures the resistance of the fabric to tear at the points around the end of the cuts (Fig 7.8).

### Seam-strength test

This tests a machine-sewn seam in an upholstery fabric. A pull-test machine is used to stretch a small sample of fabric which has been folded in half and sewn across at 12mm (½in) from the fold (Fig 7.9). There are a number of possible results: the seam may gape, or slip, or the thread used for sewing may fracture. Such tests are varied to test different sewing threads and a variety of needles and stitch-length settings.

### Fire test

This tests an upholstery fabric for its resistance to ignition by various fire applications. These include a burning cigarette, the match test, a butane gas flame

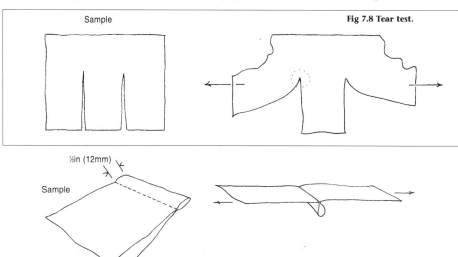

Sample

**Fig 7.8 Tear test.**

½in (12mm)

Sample

**Fig 7.9 Seam-strength test.**

and the wood crib. The Furniture and Furnishings (Fire) (Safety) Regulations 1988, and amendments, gives further details of the tests (*see* pages 12–13).

## Labelling

When it is purchased, the fabric should have a ticket or label containing most, if not all, of the following information:

- Fabric name and type
- Code number followed by a colourway number
- Fibre content as a percentage of the whole content
- Width of the cloth in centimetres
- Its suitability for use
- The colourways available
- The pattern repeat size, if any
- The price, including a piece price and a cut-length price per metre

Furnishing fabrics usually fall into four different categories of use: curtain weights, loose cover materials, upholstery fabrics, and cushions and bedspreads. A colour-coding system is often used on the label to indicate into which category a fabric falls.

Upholstery grade fabrics are grouped into five different areas of duty: occasional use, light domestic, general domestic, severe domestic or general contract, and severe contract. The suitability of a fabric, in this respect, is commonly indicated on the label.

## Ordering fabrics

### Colour matching

Every effort is made by fabric manufacturers to match pattern books and samples, but they cannot guarantee to match a shade exactly. If a fabric has to be matched then a sample should be sent or a stock cutting can be requested. Always try to order the full amount of fabric required, or wait until it is available, since buying in part at different times may result in slight shade variations.

### Inspection

Orders for upholstery fabrics are supplied on the understanding that the goods will be carefully inspected prior to cutting or processing. Errors can be made, and damage can occur in transit. Always check before cutting that the length supplied is correct in all aspects. Exchanges cannot be made once a length has been cut (*see* pages 28–9).

### Special colours

As well as the stock range offered, special colours in most designs are available for quantity orders.

### Old designs

Although a cloth may be withdrawn and not listed, many suppliers continue to hold old stock. Always check.

## Working with fabrics

The following are some rules that are worth remembering when working with fabrics:

1. Always make allowance for shrinkage and movement when making up loose cover and detachable covers.
2. Applied finishes may help fabric resist soil and stain.
3. Fabric is not a stable material and so the pattern may not always be square upon the cloth.
4. When cutting plain-dyed and woven fabric, follow the weft threads across the width.
5. Printed designs should be cut by following the pattern or design across the piece, ignoring the weave.

## Storage of covers

While work is in progress it pays to take good care of fabrics, hides and vinyls so that the possibility of damage or soiling is minimized. A large sheet of calico makes a good dust cover when a piece of work is to be left unattended or overnight.

Storage of covers is important both before and after cutting. Rolls of cover of any kind, but particularly velvet and vinyls, should never be left standing on end for very long. Keeping a cover folded for any length of time can cause crease and crush lines, which on hides, vinyls and pile fabrics particularly, can result in permanent lines or marks. Cut cover parts are best rolled loosely or laid flat on a large shelf or a side table.

Fabrics must be protected from the sun. Window glass magnifies the destructive elements in sunlight. Winter sun and reflections from snow are even more harmful than summer sun.

## Cleaning fabrics

Use a reputable dry-cleaner who specializes in home furnishings. Very few upholstery fabrics are washable.

Fixed covers should be regularly brushed or gently hoovered. To remove dirt, use a special upholstery shampoo and follow the maker's instructions. Do not use strong detergents or bleach.

Note the international textile care labelling code:

### Hand wash

| | | |
|---|---|---|
| Warm |  | Cold Rinse |
| Minimum Wash | | Short spin – do not wring |

Do not wash

### Drying
Drip dry: for best results whilst wet

Line dry: for best results hang damp

### Bleaching
When this symbol appears on a label, household bleach must not be used.

### Ironing

The number of dots in the ironing symbol indicates the correct temperature setting – the fewer the dots the cooler the iron setting.

 cool    warm    hot   ⊠ do not iron

### Dry-cleaning

Must be dry-cleaned professionally. Do not 'coin-op' clean.

Do not dry-clean

### Notes

Velvet, chenille and all heavyweight fabrics such as tapestry, matelassé and brocade should be dry-cleaned. Fabrics with a back-coated, flame-resistant finish also need to be dry-cleaned.

**Acrylics**  The dry-cleaners need to be clearly warned when a fabric includes acrylic yarns. Permanent damage may occur at temperatures exceeding 40°C. The ℗ sensitive process should always be used.

**Glazed chintz**  In order to preserve its characteristic sheen, glazed chintz should be dry-cleaned or hand-washed. If washing by hand, avoid rubbing and twisting, and keep fabric as flat as possible to minimize creasing.

## Advising the customer

The customer should be given the following advice on fabric care:

1   Regular soft brushing or vacuum cleaning will keep covers in good condition. Fabrics are weakened by dust and grit.
2   The wearing qualities of upholstery fabrics vary enormously depending on the strength of the yarn and the weaving technique. Most fabric suppliers grade their range of covers for wear.
3   Pile fabrics such as velvet may flatten when people sit on them. This is mostly inevitable and does not affect the durability of the fabric.
4   Leather will age and crease attractively but will need cleaning from time to time. A leather manufacturer's instruction sheet is recommended.
5   Wherever possible, removable cushions should be plumped and rotated to keep furniture looking good and to spread the wear. Fabrics are damaged by direct heat and strong sunlight which weakens fibres and fades the colours.
6   Arm caps should be recommended on upholstered furniture.
7   Loose threads should never be pulled or cut but carefully threaded and needled back into the upholstery.
8   Spillages and stains should be dealt with quickly but don't use anything wetter than a damp cloth. Soaking an upholstery cloth can leave a permanent mark or cause puckering or damage to the interior.
9   Fabric labels will usually state that a cover can be cleaned by standard cleaning methods, or it may detail suggested ways of removing stains, or simply state that a cover should be dry-cleaned only. Methods of cleaning depend mainly on whether a cover is fixed or detachable.

# CHAPTER 8

# Trimmings and Decoration

## Decorative Nails and Nailing

Upholstery nails have been used by the upholsterer for well over 250 years (see page 37). The early upholstery of leather-covered oak chairs had large raised head nails to fix and hold the leather in place and decorate chair edges. Today, fixings are more sophisticated and the upholstery nail is only used as a decoration and finish in traditional and reproduction work.

**Fig 8.2 Nailing techniques.**

**Fig 8.1 (above) Upholstery nail-head designs.**

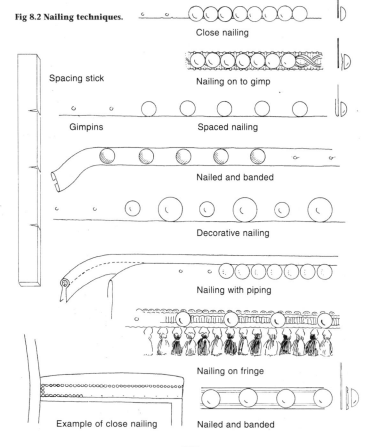

Close nailing

Spacing stick

Nailing on to gimp

Gimpins

Spaced nailing

Nailed and banded

Decorative nailing

Nailing with piping

Nailing on fringe

Example of close nailing

Nailed and banded

Standard-size nails are about ⅜in (10mm) diameter with a ¾in (19mm) leg length. Surface treatment of the domed heads can vary from plain brass to intricate design, embossed pattern and enamelled paint finishes. Nails can be bought singly or in boxes of 1000. A range of examples follows:

⅜, ¾ or ⅞in (10, 19 or 22mm) antique on steel, polished brass, antique brass, antique on brass, electro brassed, Oxford hammered, speckled old gold, French natural, bronze renaissance, honeycomb, daisy, ¼in (6mm) nickel-plated or brassed, ⅜in (9mm) enamelled, all colours.

A variety of nailing techniques are used (Fig 8.2). Close nailing is often used in hide work and is noticeable on much mid- to late-18th-century upholstery. French furniture of the late 19th century and early 20th century was often close nailed on to braids and fringes.

Space-nailed finishes, with or without bandings, can be seen on many examples of Victorian and Edwardian furniture. Bandings for use with nailing can be made up by firms specializing in leather work, from cut and folded strips of leather offcuts. These are made to standard widths to suit nail sizes and are usually tooled with two embossed lines.

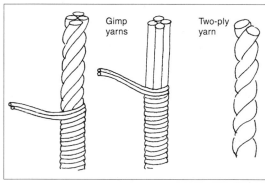

**Fig 8.3 Gimp and braid.**

Scroll gimp

Coronation gimp

Argyle gimp

Oxford gimp

Border gimp

Braid

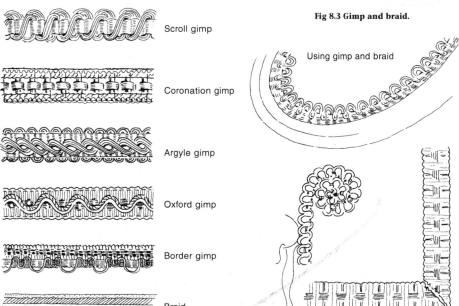

Using gimp and braid

# Trimmings

Functional and decorative proprietary trimmings are used to enhance, close and disguise tacked and stitched edges. They can also be added simply as a form of traditional decoration. Woven trimmings were traditionally made from silk, wool or cotton, with sometimes the addition of fancy yarns or threads in gold, silver and other metals. Today the majority of trimmings are woven from synthetic yarns, particularly acetate and viscose rayons.

## Gimp and braid (Fig 8.3)

Gimp and braid are narrow, woven fabrics produced on trimming machinery. The term gimp, however, is the method of making a fancy yarn by wrapping a group of threads with a number of other threads in a fine spiral. This forms a very narrow cord, and it is from this that gimp and braid trimmings are woven. Braids and gimps vary in width from ⅜ to 1in (10–25mm).

## Trimming cord (Fig 8.4)

Trimming cord (or upholstery cord) is a decorative silk cord, made up from different fancy yarns, some of which are gimp yarns, and others which are two- and three-ply twisted

**Fig 8.4 Trimming cord.**

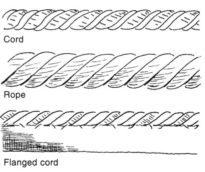

Cord

Rope

Flanged cord

Two-cord twist

**Fig 8.5 Chair ruches.**

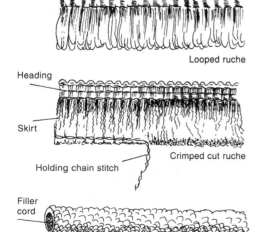

Looped ruche

Heading

Skirt

Crimped cut ruche

Holding chain stitch

Filler cord

Berry ruche

yarns. By combining these, some very interesting effects are achieved, particularly when different colours are used. Trimming cords vary in thickness from ³⁄₁₆ to ⅜in (5–10mm) in diameter.

## Ruche (Fig 8.5)

Ruche is a narrow woven or knitted fabric with a heavy multiple weft to form a ruche edge, rather like a miniature fringe. There are three types – looped ruche, cut ruche and berry ruche – and they are all flanged to provide an edge for fixing or sewing into a seam.

**Fig 8.6 Fringe.**

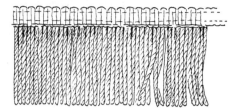

Rope fringe

## Fringe (Fig 8.6)

Fringe is another narrow, woven fabric, with cut or looped weft threads. These hang or extend beyond the warps to form a decorative edge. The weft threads forming the fringe are sometimes bunched or knotted together to produce different effects. Fringe is made up of a heading and a skirt, and may also have tassels and balls added for effect and decoration. Fringes are used as an edging which may be glued, pinned or sewn, mainly to chair bases.

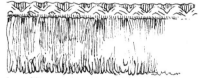

Loop fringe

## Bandings

Bandings are narrow strips of leather or plastic-coated fabric, folded and glued into a flat band of about ½in (13mm) width. They are designed to be fixed with studs or upholstery nails around edges, facings, etc., and are mostly used in leather work, or with vinyl-coated fabrics.

Tassel fringe

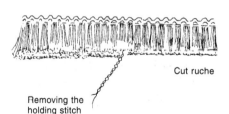

Cut ruche

Removing the holding stitch

# Tassels

The tassel used in furnishing has a turned wooden core or moulé which forms the basis of the tassel head and its shape. The head may be overwound vertically or horizontally with fine yarn and a winding used if there is a waisted shape. Glues and wires are then used to hold and finish the various parts in place.

A simplified version of the tassel can be made using a length of upholstery cord, a wooden bead and several metres of embroidery thread or coloured cotton yarn. The yarns are tied very tightly above the bead with two thirds of their length above the tie. The yarns are arranged evenly around the bead and the pulled into a waisted tassel shape under the bead. The waist is held and fixed with a horizontal winding to a good depth and knotted off.

**Fig 8.7 Tassels.**

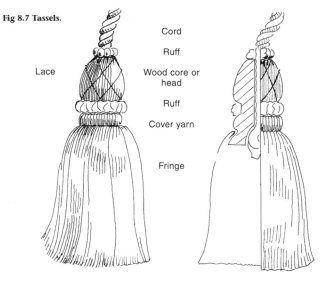

Cord

Ruff

Lace

Wood core or head

Ruff

Cover yarn

Fringe

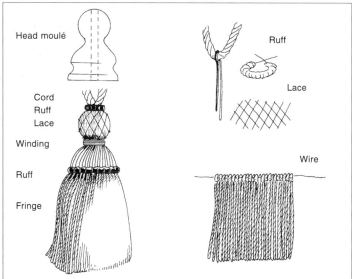

Head moulé

Cord
Ruff
Lace

Winding

Ruff

Fringe

Ruff

Lace

Wire

# Tufts

Tufts are generally circular and measure about ¾in (20mm) across with a strong cord or twine stitched through the back ready for needling into a piece of work.

A winding stick for tuft-making is a simple tool made from ¼in (6mm) thick hardwood with curved, smooth faces, softly rounded edges and a saw cut or

**Fig 8.8 Tufts.**

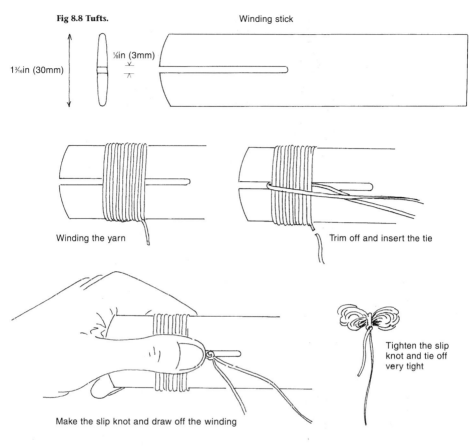

Winding stick

⅛in (3mm)

1³⁄₁₆in (30mm)

Winding the yarn

Trim off and insert the tie

Make the slip knot and draw off the winding

Tighten the slip knot and tie off very tight

groove. Twenty complete turns will produce a good thick tuft which is pulled in and knotted at its centre. The tighter the centre tie is tied, the more rounded and splayed the tuft yarns will become. A fine strong mattress twine can be needled into the back of the tuft for tying into the work.

In Fig 8.8, A and B show an end and a face view of the completed tuft, while C shows how the tuft is slightly reduced in size and closed up when pulled tightly into place; D is a square-shaped tuft made from cotton cord and drawn from an original, taken from a chair which was designed and made in the late nineteenth century.

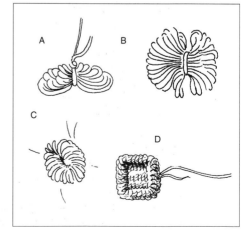

A   B

C   D

# Cabbages and Rosettes

Fig 8.9 shows three typical applications of cabbages and rosettes. In the top example the cabbage appears as a centre piece on the pleated ceiling of a four-poster bed, neatly concealing the wires on to which the drapery has been pleated.

Fig 8.10 shows the dimensions for making up two kinds of cabbage and a rosette to a finished size of approximately 2in (50mm).

CABBAGES

2in
(50mm)

2in
(50mm)

5½in
(140mm)

5½in
(140mm)

**Fig 8.9 (above) Three examples of
how cabbages and rosettes are used.**

**Fig 8.10 Two varieties of cabbage, and a rosette.**

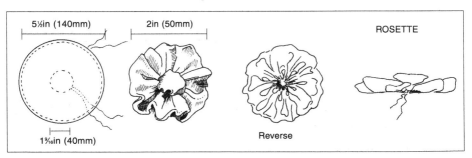

5½in (140mm)

2in (50mm)

ROSETTE

Reverse

1⅝in (40mm)

# Valances

Shown in Fig 8.11 are some variations of the plain valance or skirt and its general construction. Dimensioning needs to be precise so that the position and fit are good. The depth of the valance is usually in proportion to the whole piece and the height is set at 1in (25mm) above the floor line when the chair or bed is standing on a firm floor. This allows for a very small amount of drop and for the depth of carpeting etc.

Valances that have been gathered, box pleated or box pleated with space are shown in Fig 8.12. The technique of fold-back corners is often used in industrial upholstery as this allows for the making up of skirting strips in quantity, which can then be set to varying lengths as they are assembled either on to a piping or back-tacked directly on to a chair.

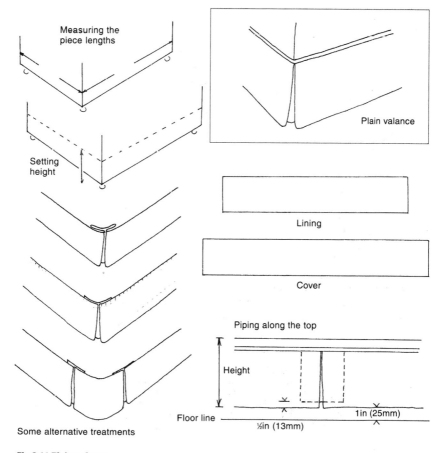

Measuring the piece lengths

Plain valance

Setting height

Lining

Cover

Piping along the top

Height

Floor line

½in (13mm)

1in (25mm)

Some alternative treatments

**Fig 8.11 Plain valance.**

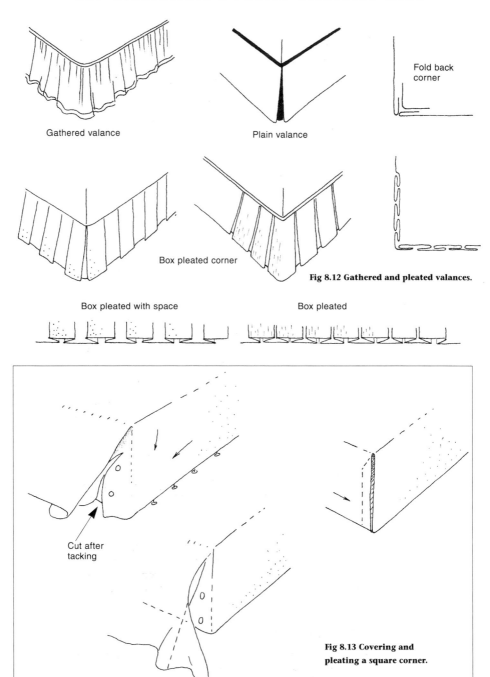

Gathered valance

Plain valance

Fold back corner

Box pleated corner

**Fig 8.12 Gathered and pleated valances.**

Box pleated with space

Box pleated

Cut after tacking

**Fig 8.13 Covering and pleating a square corner.**

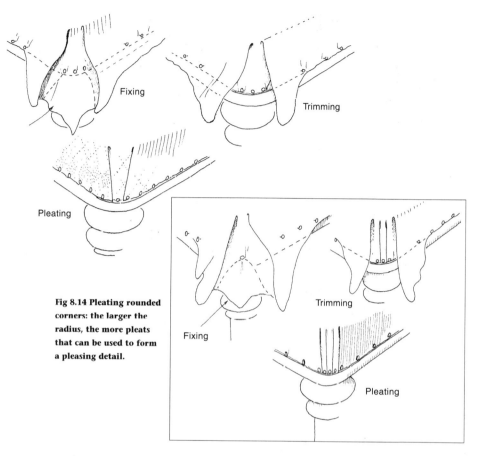

Fixing

Trimming

Pleating

**Fig 8.14 Pleating rounded corners: the larger the radius, the more pleats that can be used to form a pleasing detail.**

Fixing

Trimming

Pleating

# Pleating, Borders and Facings

## Pleating

Pleating is a technique used in upholstery covering to absorb the fullness in fabrics and to give accent to a corner or scroll. The underlying shape of the upholstery will determine exactly how the pleating should be arranged and how many folds are necessary to take out all the fullness. An odd number of pleats or folds will often look more pleasing than an even number.

## Borders and facings

Dimensions are of course variable but ½in (13mm) pleats will give a fully pleated effect. Needlework boxes, cupboard linings and glazed door panels were often decorated with fabrics in this way from the middle of the last century.

A plain border with piped edge. The piping can be contrast or self-piped, and is usually machine sewn and capped on.

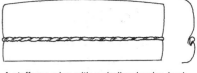

A stuffover edge with a shallow border, back-tacked with a flanged cord.

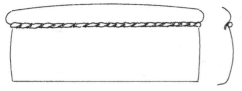

An under-edge seat front with a deep border slip-stitched below the lip. The sewing line is disguised with an upholstery cord hand-sewn under the edge.

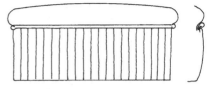

A pleated border machine sewn to an under-edge seat panel with a piped seam. The piping flange is either carefully hand-stitched into the seat, or back-tacked to a firm edge before the border is filled and pulled down.

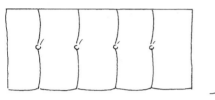

A purely decorative pleated and buttoned border typical of Victorian upholstery. This is used on seat fronts and also arm and back edges. It is more effective if small (size 20) buttons are used.

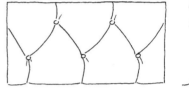

A half-diamond buttoned and pleated border. A reasonable depth of filling is needed to produce a good result.

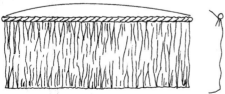

The ruched border is tightly gathered and then hand stitched to the top of a firm edge, e.g. a stitched edge. Upholstery cord sits snugly over the seam. This is typical of late Victorian and Edwardian upholstery.

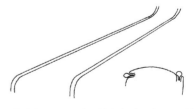

A plain, narrow piped border hand or machine sewn to chair arms and wings, etc. This gives a clean and even finish to the edges of headboards and Edwardian drawing room chairs.

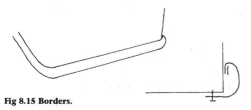

A simple and effective method of enhancing and finishing the outline of a chair frame base. The small padded border is back-tacked about ¾in (20mm) high, with either a light or heavy filling.

**Fig 8.15 Borders.**

# Pipings

Pipings can vary enormously in their size and make up, from fine ⅛in (3mm) welts for leather work to the large, soft foam-filled pipings for some modern work. The traditional method of make up is still used as the best way of producing a prominent edge and a strong seam line. Sizes will usually depend on the cord available and the size of the machine piping feet that can be bought or specially made up. The following are those most commonly used: ⅛in (3mm); 3⁄16in (4.5mm); ¼in (6.3mm); 5⁄16in (8mm) and ⅜in (9.5mm). Machine presser feet in the

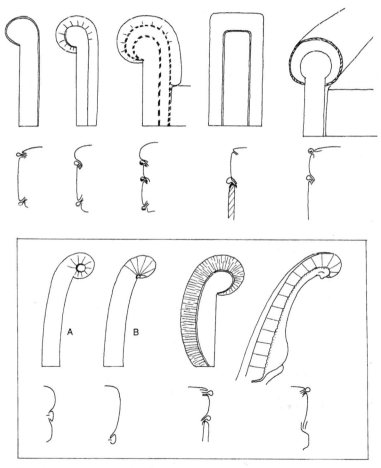

A          B

**Fig 8.16 A selection of facings and their construction. A and B are not strictly applied facings but rather a manipulation of the inside arm fabric to produce pleating designs. Each is finished with a button or a medallion, and is in the French style; the other facings shown are mainly traditional English styles.**

**Fig 8.17 Gathering, ruching and pleating. These techniques can be used on borders and facings to produce depth of texture and colour.**

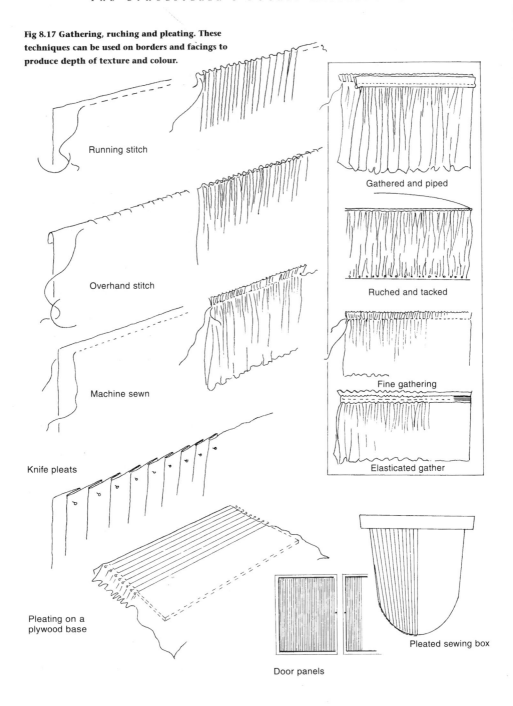

Running stitch

Overhand stitch

Machine sewn

Knife pleats

Pleating on a plywood base

Gathered and piped

Ruched and tacked

Fine gathering

Elasticated gather

Door panels

Pleated sewing box

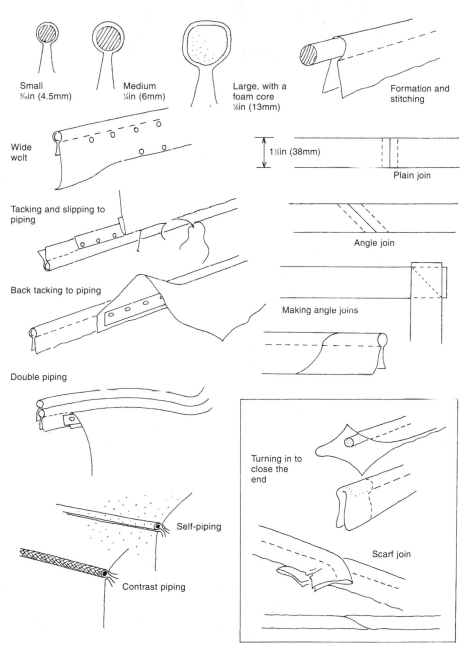

Small
³⁄₁₆in (4.5mm)

Medium
¼in (6mm)

Large, with a
foam core
½in (13mm)

Formation and
stitching

Wide
welt

1½in (38mm)

Plain join

Tacking and slipping to
piping

Angle join

Back tacking to piping

Making angle joins

Double piping

Turning in to
close the
end

Self-piping

Contrast piping

Scarf join

**Fig 8.18 Pipings.**

form of half feet can be used for the larger soft-filled variations using foam or polyester fibre as fillings.

Conventionally made piping, or welt as it is known in industrial upholstery, gives a fine but flexible corded strip for sewing or upholstering into a chair cover.

In cushion making, the bias-cut piping with a washable cotton twist cord insert remains the favourite. It is versatile, tough and has a stretch and flexibility which gives the final seam a good-looking and well-behaved edge. The bias-cut fabric strip helps particularly on curved work and also where there are no rigid fixings. The bias-cut direction in a cover is at 45° to the edge, thus making the cuts more expensive than straight-cut strips. Straight-cut strips of cover for piping can usually make use of waste areas and edges and so are relatively economical in cover use.

Large soft welts or pipings can be made up using narrow-cut strips of foam or polyester fibre fillings. These are typical applications in modern upholstery and may be as large as ¾in (20mm) across. This kind of piping is used around cushions and facings to give a soft and pronounced outline to the shape and design of a chair.

## Estimating for piping (see page 153)

**Across the width**

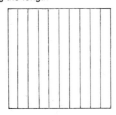

**Along the length**

**On the bias**

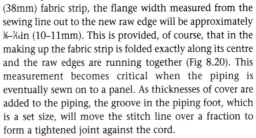

**Fig 8.19 Methods of cutting piping strips.**
**Piping strips: 1½in (38mm).**

There are three different ways to cut piping strips from a fabric or cover: across the width, along the length or on the bias (Fig 8.19). Each produces a slightly different kind of piping and each behaves differently when it is made up and in use. Grain, weave and direction of cut all affect its feel and its flexibility.

The width of piping or welt strip is 1½in (38mm). This is a good average width and is suitable for making up with piping cords of ⅛, ¼ and ⁵⁄₁₆in (4, 6 and 7.5mm). When piping thicknesses go beyond these sizes then a little more width in the strip will be needed.

When a piping of average size is made up and sewn from a 1½in (38mm) fabric strip, the flange width measured from the sewing line out to the new raw edge will be approximately ⅜–⁷⁄₁₆in (10–11mm). This is provided, of course, that in the making up the fabric strip is folded exactly along its centre and the raw edges are running together (Fig 8.20). This measurement becomes critical when the piping is eventually sewn on to a panel. As thicknesses of cover are added to the piping, the groove in the piping foot, which is a set size, will move the stitch line over a fraction to form a tightened joint against the cord.

During assembly, the second and third sewings will take up the ⅜–⁷⁄₁₆in (10–11mm) sewing allowance automatically, on a panel or a border to which the piping is being sewn.

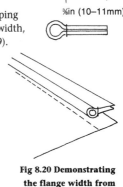

⅜in (10–11mm)

**Fig 8.20 Demonstrating the flange width from the sewing line to the raw edge for an average-sized piping.**

# Buttoning and Fluting

## Buttoning

Surface buttoning and deep buttoning have been used since the Victorian era to fix and decorate fabrics into chair seats and backs. During the 1950s, surface buttoning again became fashionable, partly as a decorative feature and also as a method of holding fabrics into a compound shaped work. Some typical surface button patterns are shown in Fig 8.21. Buttons also increased in size, from the small farthing-sized Victorian buttons to large machine-made buttons about 2in (50mm) across.

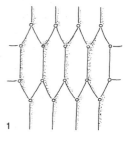
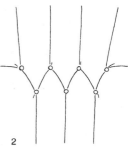

### Buttoning layouts

There are two general rules which apply to most button layouts and will help to obtain good balanced results:

1  The outer buttons on all sides of the pattern should not be placed too close to the edges. The distance usually depends on the size and shape of the piece of work. Very generally, 2½–3½in (63–90mm) is an average spacing. On the other hand, buttoning which is set too far in from the edges will look lost and unprofessional.

2  The shape of the layout should, as far as possible, conform to the general proportions and shape of the piece being buttoned. In the same way, the size of the diamonds should be in keeping with the overall size of the area being buttoned. The following examples will give a useful guide: 4½ x 2½in (114 x 63mm) and 5 x 3in (125 x 75mm) are small diamonds and will suit dining chairs and sewing chairs. 6 x 4in (150 x 100mm) diamonds are about medium sized and would be correct for larger seats and backs of lounge chairs, chaises longues and headboards for beds. Anything above these sizes, for example 7 x 5in (175 x 125mm) or 8 x 6in (200 x 150mm), would look well on sofas, settees and large wing chairs.

**Fig 8.22 Traditional diamond buttoning patterns.**

**Fig 8.21 Modern surface buttoning patterns using sewing lines and buttons for effect.**

Fig 8.22 shows three alternative layouts which can be used in chair backs to produce effective patterns:

1  The centre row of buttons is left out, to create short flutes

2  A row of half diamonds with long pleats radiating vertically

3  Diamonds which reduce in size to suit a waisted frame

## Measuring cover for buttoning

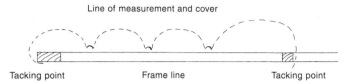

Line of measurement and cover

Tacking point        Frame line        Tacking point

**Fig 8.23 (above) One method of measuring cover for buttoning. The length and width can be found by laying a linen tape measure across the prepared top stuffing from one tacking point to the other, taking the line with the most button positions. The tape is then gently pushed down into each hole allowing a generous depth at each button position.**

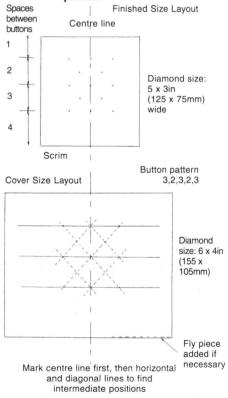

Spaces between buttons

Finished Size Layout

Centre line

1
2
3
4

Diamond size:
5 x 3in
(125 x 75mm)
wide

Scrim

Cover Size Layout

Button pattern
3,2,3,2,3

Diamond
size: 6 x 4in
(155 x 105mm)

Fly piece added if necessary

Mark centre line first, then horizontal and diagonal lines to find intermediate positions

**Fig 8.24 A second method is to measure directly from one tacking point to the other and then add a buttoning allowance figure – 1¼in (32mm) is a typical average allowance – for every space between buttons along the line being measured.**

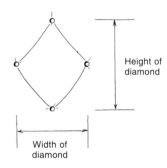

Height of diamond

Width of diamond

## Buttoning allowance

Before button positions can be decided upon, a buttoning allowance must be made, in order to give depth to the buttons and produce the pleats or folds which form the diamond pattern. The amount of allowance made depends on the depth of buttoning required and the size of the individual diamond patterns. The allowances for deep buttoning are simply the difference between the diamond size on the scrim and the diamond size measured over the stuffing and down into the holes. This extra is then added to the width and height of the diamonds when they are marked on to the reverse side of the cover.

The following gives some typical diamond sizes and their allowances:

| Scrim size diamond | Allowance | Cover size diamond | Approx. depth of stuffing |
|---|---|---|---|
| 4½in x 2½in (114mm x 63mm) | 1in (25mm) | 5½in x 3½in (140mm x 90mm) | 1¾in (45mm) |
| 5in x 3in (125mm x 75mm) | 1¼in (32mm) | 6¼in x 4¼in (160mm x 108mm) | 2in (50mm) |
| 6in x 4in (150mm x 100mm) | 1½in (38mm) | 7½in x 5½in (190mm x 140mm) | 2½in (63mm) |
| 7in x 5in (175mm x 125mm) | 1¾in (45mm) | 8¾in x 6¾in (222mm x 170mm) | 3in (75mm) |

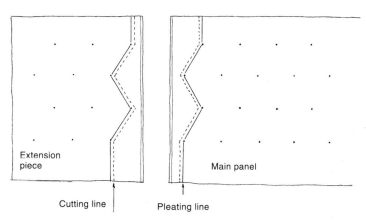

Extension piece

Main panel

Cutting line

Pleating line

**Fig 8.26 A vandyked joint is used to widen fabrics for deep buttoning.**

## Vandyking

The jointing of leather by hand in a zig-zag line in buttoning work was traditionally called vandyking. But today the term is more generally used to describe the sewn joint used to widen any covering in buttoning work (Fig 8.26)

The join follows the line of pleating between buttons, and once the buttoning is in place, the joint line is no longer visible.

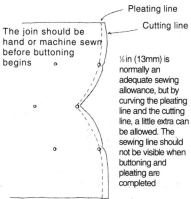

Pleating line

Cutting line

The join should be hand or machine sewn before buttoning begins

½in (13mm) is normally an adequate sewing allowance, but by curving the pleating line and the cutting line, a little extra can be allowed. The sewing line should not be visible when buttoning and pleating are completed

# Fluting

Fluted upholstery is sometimes called channel work. It may be defined as a series of separately filled sections arranged in vertical, horizontal or curved lines, each divided by hand- or machine-sewn seams. Fluted upholstery design is commonly used on chair backs, cushions and bed headboards (Fig 8.27).

A fluted panel is made up of a base cloth of hessian or calico, a layer of soft filling and a top cover. The panel can either be built directly on to a ready sprung first-stuffed base, or machine-made then filled and applied as a pre-formed component (Fig 8.28).

In modern upholstery, the depth of stitching required for fluting is created by machine sewing through a cover and a soft padding of foam or other filling. A good combination is foam and polyester fibre. The depth of work depends on the type or thickness of the filling being used.

Producing this type of work on a standard lock-stitch sewing machine means being restricted to small panels. Large fluted panels have to be made on long-arm sewing machines, specially designed for this kind of work (see page 32).

Fluted panels tend to be produced for fixing into upholstered chairs and are incorporated into the upholstery by sewing or stapling (Fig 8.29).

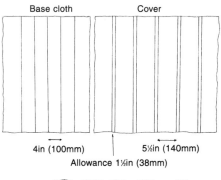

**Fig 8.27 Fluted upholstery designs.**

**Fig 8.28 Making up fluted panels.**

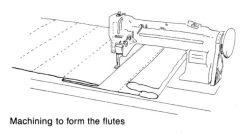

Machining to form the flutes

Base cloth    Cover

4in (100mm)    5¼in (140mm)

Allowance 1½in (38mm)

End view showing cover folded and sewn to base cloth

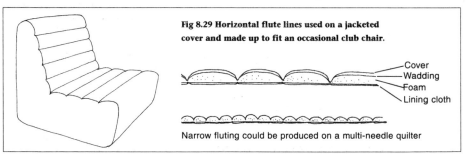

**Fig 8.29 Horizontal flute lines used on a jacketed cover and made up to fit an occasional club chair.**

Cover
Wadding
Foam
Lining cloth

Narrow fluting could be produced on a multi-needle quilter

# CHAPTER 9

# Calculations

## Cover Cutting Plans and Parts

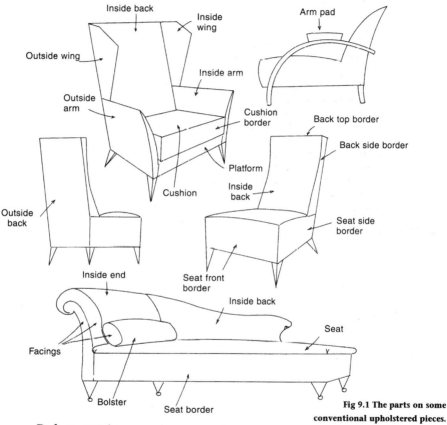

Fig 9.1 The parts on some conventional upholstered pieces.

### Before cutting

It is the responsibility of the upholsterer to make a thorough inspection of a cover before it is cut (see page 28). The following is a useful checklist:

1   Is the fabric the one that was ordered?
2   Are the length and width as specified?
3   Is the colour correct and as per the sample?
4   Has it got damaged or dirty in transit?
5   Are there any faults or flaws in the fabric?

Some faults which often occur are bad creasing or crushing, yarns drifting and not square to the selvedge, large knots, missing or broken yarns, distortion or bareness in pile fabrics, changes in density, and bad registration in printed covers.

If a flaw is found by the manufacturer, then he will sew a brightly coloured yarn alongside it into the selvedge to indicate that a flaw is present, and that an extra half metre has been allowed on the length.

## Railroading

Fig 9.2 shows a comparison between the conventional layout of fabric on to chairs and settees and the 'railroad' technique. In large-scale production of upholstered furniture, the technique of running fabric along the length of large pieces of furniture, called railroading, can be more economical in the fabric used, and will also save time in matching and joining.

**Fig 9.2 Railroading.**

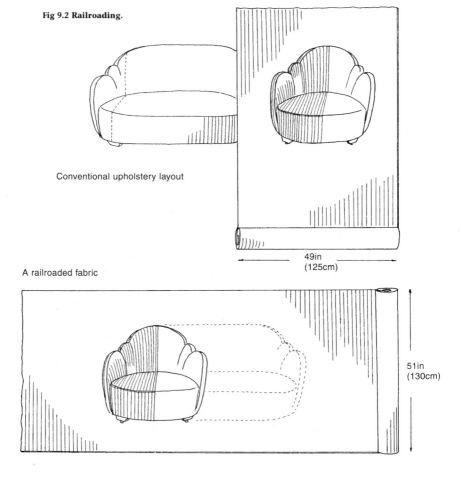

Conventional upholstery layout

49in
(125cm)

A railroaded fabric

51in
(130cm)

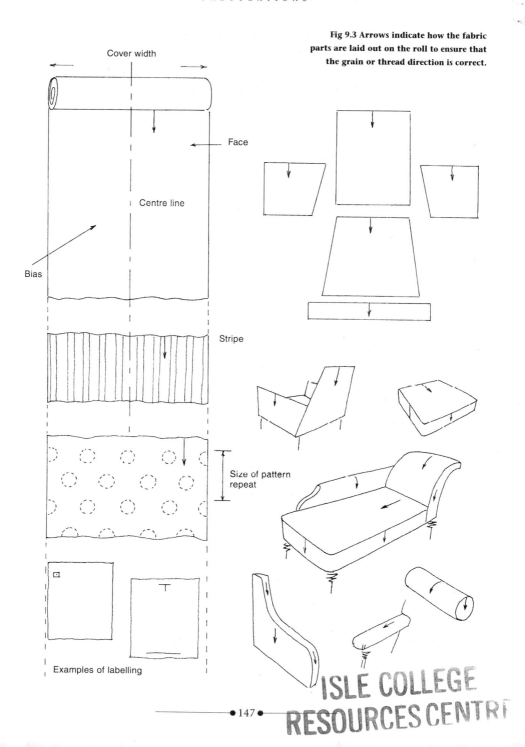

**Fig 9.3 Arrows indicate how the fabric parts are laid out on the roll to ensure that the grain or thread direction is correct.**

Cover width

Face

Centre line

Bias

Stripe

Size of pattern repeat

Examples of labelling

The system calls for special fabrics to be made so that patterns will be upright when a fabric is used sideways on. However, this is still a very specialized area of upholstery manufacture, and the bulk of fabrics used for furnishing remain of the conventional type, unsuitable for this kind of treatment, with an average width of 125cm (49in) and with repeats of the pattern running up and down the roll length.

A number of different plain surface coverings can be adapted to the railroad system quite easily, e.g. vinyl-coated cloths, plain wool tweeds and suede nylon cloths.

## Marking out and fitting covers and fabrics

When marking out the cover for a piece of upholstery, measurements have to be kept within the parameters of the cover: the cover width and length, and any texture, pile, pattern or design. With the fabric laid out on a cutting table, face side up, the arrangement and particular treatment of the covering can be visualized.

Grain or thread direction must also be considered, as it is very important to 'cut to thread' in both the warp and the weft directions. In some fabrics the grain will be strong and very obvious, whereas in others, e.g. velours and printed fabrics, it is hidden below the pile or colouring.

A mental check list is useful:

1  Is the face side of the cover obvious? The fabric should have been rolled up with the face inside.
2  Which is the top (or bottom) of the surface design or pattern?
3  Check the grain or thread of the cover, and trim the leading edge straight with the thread before starting to mark out and cut.
4  Does the fabric have a pile, and is the pile direction obvious? If not, lay a small coin on the surface and tap the table; the coin will travel in the direction of the pile.
5  What is the size of the pattern repeat, and how does it relate to the main areas and sizes to be cut?
6  Check the position of stripes or cords in the cover, and choose a centre which can be used throughout the job.
7  What does the half-width measure and how does it tie up with the sizes to be cut? Can the half width be used to advantage so that cover parts will match across and be mirrored?
8  Will there be extension pieces to be added to the width or half width, and where will they conveniently come from?
9  Is the centre of the fabric obvious, and can it be chosen now?
10  Are stripes dominant? If so, how can they be best placed for effect?
11  Should any bold stripes be used or avoided for small parts such as facings and buttons?
12  Where will pipings be cut from?
13  Can unseen cushion borders be cut from oddments for economy?
14  Are fly pieces being used to make savings on the cover?

Upholstery covers are best marked out on the face side so that the features of the cloth are always visible.

**Fig 9.4 Two cutting plans for the same chair.**

For a plain cover

For a patterned cover with a dominant central motif

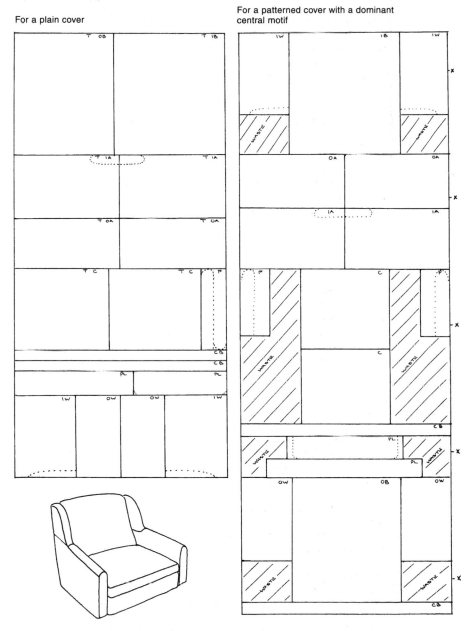

Woven and printed patterns become very important when they are bold and large, as they will be central to the main areas of the work, e.g. inside backs and seats. Smaller, all-over patterns and fine stripes are generally not as dominant and therefore more flexible in the cutting layout; however, it is usually advisable to select a centre line early on and to stick to it throughout the layout.

Plain covers are of course much more flexible and easier to deal with, but the same code of practice should be followed as a matter of habit, especially when face side and grain direction are being checked.

White, dust-free chalk is an ideal marking medium, and, when used with light pressure, allows for adjustments if errors are made. Tailor's crayon is also used extensively, but this is more difficult to remove.

## Labelling

Once a length of fabric has been cut into smaller parts, each part should be labelled so that all parts remain in order and ready for use without delay or confusion. Pairs can be kept together and those parts to be matched or sewn can be pinned. There are various ways of labelling parts:

1   Labelling in industry is done with chalk on the reverse side of the cover: the top is marked with a large 'T', and the positions of flies and extensions are marked with a thick straight line just inside the edge. Where two pieces are to be sewn into shapes, edges are marked with V-notches as balance marks.
2   Labelling can be done with pins, which are always placed in the same position on each piece, e.g. the top left or bottom left corners.
3   Small slips of paper can be used, marked with the part's name and always pinned in the same place.

## Marking and cutting sequence

If space is limited, covers can be marked piecemeal and parts cut when they are needed. The best sequence in this case will depend on the type of work being done: for chair work, the inside arm pieces and inside backs will generally be needed first, followed by, for example, the inside wings and then the seat cover. Cushion panels and borders should be marked out and cut together, and then rolled up until needed.

## Accuracy

Cover parts to be upholstered and tacked into place will need an allowance of 2–3in (52–75mm) for pulling and tacking down. This fairly generous amount can be carefully reduced where the positioning is precise and the part is relatively small.

Where cover parts are to be fitted or are shaped ready for machine sewing, the allowances need to be much smaller and more accurate: ⅜in or ½in (10 or 13mm) is normally the maximum margin, and must be accurately kept to during marking and cutting. The machinist automatically follows an imaginary line of this margin just inside and parallel to the edge of the fabric. Most sewing work of this kind in upholstery is done with an allowance of ⅜in (10mm). Occasionally allowances are varied for certain difficult coverings, e.g. ½in (13mm) for very loosely woven fabrics, and reduced to ¼in (6mm) for some leather work.

# Measuring

Measurements for a cover can be taken from a bare frame or, in the case of new work, from a full-size drawing or a made-up prototype. In the case of reupholstery, the measuring for cover can be done directly from the existing upholstery, with any allowances made for changes in shape or upholstery design.

If possible the type of covering should be known, so that sewn joints can be placed or matched correctly, or avoided. For some plain coverings, however, especially those with little or no texture or surface grain, the cover is often placed in such a way as to be as economical as possible. The same treatment applies when using leather because this has no directional preference, and can be laid on to the work in the most economical way.

As far as possible, the weft yarns in a woven fabric are kept parallel to the floor. Thus the opposite warp yarns will run up and down or vertically to the floor. In the majority of woven covers the warp yarns are the stronger and therefore the more stable, and the covers will wear and drape better if laid on in this direction. On this basis, measurements can be made and the 'lay' of the cover kept in mind along with the cover width.

The length or linear measurement is the most important dimension to be established. Because material and fabric widths (measured across the roll) are set sizes, it is the length (measured up the roll) which must be worked out and planned for. However, it is good practice to check and measure the width of any material before any other measuring or marking is done. If the width of the cover is 55in (140cm), then the half-width measurement will be 27½in (70cm). This dimension should not include the selvedge.

As the measurements are taken they can be recorded and where possible fitted into the half width and paired with the opposite half width. This can usually be done with inside arm covers, outside arm covers, wing parts, cushion panels, etc.

Finally, when all the parts have been measured and notes made, the length measurements are added together, excluding those that are paired, and a total length calculated down one side of the cutting plan.

For a table of commonly used metric/imperial conversions, see page 152. A metreage chart for common-sized pieces of upholstered furniture appears on page 153.

# Calculations and Conversion Tables

**Some typical upholstery materials and their common widths**

|  | inches | millimetres |  | inches | millimetres |
|---|---|---|---|---|---|
| rubber webbings | 1½, 2 | 37, 50 | ticking | 82 | 2080 |
| woven webbings | 2 | 50 | linings | 48, 54 | 1200, 1350 |
| India tape | ½, 1 | 13, 25 | scrims | 36, 72 | 900, 1800 |
| hessians | 36, 54, 72 | 900, 1350, 1800 | calico | 36, 72 | 900, 1800 |
| canvases | 36, 39 | 900, 1000 | upholstery fabrics | 48, 50, 54 | 1200, 1270, 1350 |
| cambric | 48, 72 | 1200, 1800 |  |  |  |

**Metric and Imperial comparisons which are used all the time**

| millimetres | inches | inches | millimetres |
|---|---|---|---|
| 6 | ¼ | ¼ | 6.35 |
| 10 | ⅜ | ⅜ | 9.525 |
| 13 | ½ | ½ | 12.7 |
| 25 | 1 | 1 | 25.4 |
| 50 | 2 | 2 | 50.8 |
| 100 | 4 | 4 | 101.6 |
| 300 | 12 | 12 | 305 |
| 900 | 36 | 36 | 914 |
| 1000 | 39⅜ | 39 | 990.6 |
| nominal sizes which are used in the workshop | | conversion when more precise sizes are needed | |

**To convert square feet to square metres or square metres to square feet**

| Square feet | | Square metres | Square feet | | Square metres |
|---|---|---|---|---|---|
| 10.764 | 1 | 0.093 | 64.584 | 6 | 0.557 |
| 21.528 | 2 | 0.186 | 75.347 | 7 | 0.650 |
| 32.292 | 3 | 0.279 | 86.111 | 8 | 0.743 |
| 43.056 | 4 | 0.372 | 96.875 | 9 | 0.836 |
| 53.820 | 5 | 0.465 | 107.64 | 10 | 0.93 |

The central column gives the key figures and can be read as either the imperial or the metric measurement. Example: one square metre is equal to 10.764 square feet, or one square foot is equal to 0.093 square metres.

| To convert | Multiply by |
|---|---|
| Cubic inches to cubic centimetres | 16.387 |
| Cubic centimetres to cubic inches | 0.06102 |
| Cubic feet to cubic metres | 0.02831 |
| Cubic metres to cubic feet | 35.3157 |
| Cubic yards to cubic metres | 0.76455 |
| Cubic metres to cubic yards | 1.30795 |

**Some nominal sizes used in the workshop:**

| | |
|---|---|
| The metric inch | 25mm |
| The metric foot | 300mm |
| The metric yard | 900mm |
| Two metric yards | 1.8m |
| 48 inches | 120cm |
| 54 inches | 135cm |
| 72 inches | 180cm |

**Metreage chart for piping lengths**

| Fabric amount | Cut/direction | Amount of piping | Strip width |
|---|---|---|---|
| Half metre (19⅝in) | Bias cut | 19m (62ft 4in) | 1½in (38mm) |
| One metre (39⅜in) | Bias cut | 38m (124ft 8in) | 1½in (38mm) |
| One and quarter metres (49¼in) | Bias cut | 47.5m (155ft 10in) | 1½in (38mm) |
| Half metre (19⅝in) | Along length | 16m (52ft 6in) | 1½in (38mm) |
| One metre (39⅜in) | Along length | 32m (105ft) | 1½in (38mm) |
| One and quarter metres (49¼in) | Along length | 40m (131ft 3in) | 1½in (38mm) |
| Half metre (19⅝in) | Across width | 16m (52ft 6in) | 1½in (38mm) |
| One metre (39⅜in) | Across width | 32m (105ft) | 1½in (38mm) |
| One and quarter metres (49¼in) | Across width | 40m (131ft 3in) | 1½in (38mm) |

**Metreage chart for common-sized pieces of upholstered furniture**

| | |
|---|---|
| Pinstuffed seats or backs | 19¾in (500mm) for 1 or 2 |
| Loose seat | 23⅝in (600mm) for 1 or 2 |
| Library chair (seat and back) | 6ft 6in (2m) |
| Stuffover seat (dining chair) | 25⅝in (650mm) |
| Prie-dieu (prayer chair) | 4ft 3in (1.3m) |
| Desk chair (swivel) | 4ft 11in (1.5m) |
| Ottoman (box only) | 3ft 11in (1.2m) |
| (with end) | 6ft 6in (2m) |
| Stool | 29½in (750mm) |
| Sewing chair | 4ft 11in (1.5m) |
| Fireside chair | 8ft 2½in (2.5m) |
| Small armchair | 11ft 10in (3.6m) |
| Large easy chair (with seat cushion) | 15ft 7in (4.75m) |
| Wing armchair (plain) | 17ft 3in (5.25m) |
| (patterned) | 19ft 8½in (6m) |
| Single-end chaise longue | 11ft 6in (3.5m) |
| Chaise longue | |
| (with end and back) | 16ft 5in (5m |
| (with buttoned end and back) | 18ft (5.5m) |
| Double-ended chaise longue | 23ft (7m) |
| Two-seater settee (fixed back) | 19ft (5.8m) |
| Two-seater settee (cushion back) | 24ft 7½in (7.5m) |
| Three-seater settee (fixed back) | 25ft 11in (7.9m) |
| Three-seater settee (cushion back) | 31ft 2in (9.5m) |
| Chesterfield (plain) | 23ft (7m) |
| (patterned) | 27ft 11in (8.5m) |

**A typical cutting list**

| Part | | Length | Width | No. |
|---|---|---|---|---|
| IB | inside back | 38 9/16in (980mm) | 27 9/16in (700mm) | 1 |
| OB | outside back | 34 5/8in (880mm) | 23 5/8in (600mm) | 1 |
| IA | inside arm | 25 19/32in (650mm) | 25 19/32in (650mm) | 2 |
| OA | outside arm | 21 21/32in (550mm) | 23 5/8in (600mm) | 2 |
| S | seat | 29 1/2in (750mm) | 31 1/2in (800mm) | 1 |
| SB | seat border | 11 13/16in (300mm) | 24 5/8in (625mm) | 1 |
| AF | arm facing | 26in (660mm) | 7 7/8in (200mm) | 2 |
| P | piping | 33ft 7 1/2in (10.25m) | 1 1/2in (38mm) | |

**Imperial standard wire gauge sizes**

| Standard wire gauge | Inches | Nearest fraction of an inch | | Nearest metric gauge |
|---|---|---|---|---|
| 7 | 0.176 | 3/16 | 0.187 | 4.5 |
| 8 | 0.160 | 5/32 | 0.156 | 4.0 |
| 9 | 0.144 | | | 3.6 |
| 10 | 0.128 | 1/8 | 0.125 | 3.3 |
| 11 | 0.116 | | | 3.0 |
| 12 | 0.104 | | | 2.7 |
| 13 | 0.092 | 3/32 | 0.093 | 2.4 |
| 14 | 0.080 | | | 2.1 |
| 15 | 0.072 | | | 1.9 |
| 16 | 0.064 | 1/16 | 0.062 | 1.65 |
| 17 | 0.056 | | | 1.45 |
| 18 | 0.048 | | | 1.25 |
| 19 | 0.040 | | | 1.05 |
| 20 | 0.036 | | | 0.95 |
| 21 | 0.032 | | | 0.85 |
| 22 | 0.028 | 1/32 | 0.031 | 0.72 |

# Conversion tables

| Length centimetres | cm or inches | inches | Weight kilograms | kg or pounds | pounds |
|---|---|---|---|---|---|
| 2.54 | 1 | 0.39 | 0.45 | 1 | 2.21 |
| 5.08 | 2 | 0.79 | 0.91 | 2 | 4.41 |
| 7.62 | 3 | 1.18 | 1.36 | 3 | 6.61 |
| 10.16 | 4 | 1.58 | 1.81 | 4 | 8.82 |
| 12.70 | 5 | 1.97 | 2.27 | 5 | 11.02 |
| 15.24 | 6 | 2.36 | 2.72 | 6 | 13.23 |
| 17.78 | 7 | 2.76 | 3.18 | 7 | 15.43 |
| 20.32 | 8 | 3.15 | 3.63 | 8 | 17.64 |
| 22.86 | 9 | 3.54 | 4.08 | 9 | 19.84 |
| 25.40 | 10 | 3.94 | 4.45 | 10 | 22.05 |

## Conversion Formulae

| To convert **Length** | Multiply by | To convert **Volume** | Multiply by |
|---|---|---|---|
| Inches to centimetres | 2.54 | Cu inches to cu centimetres | 16.387 |
| Centimetres to inches | 0.3937 | Cu centimetres to cu inches | 0.06102 |
| Feet to metres | 0.3048 | Cu feet to cu metres | 0.02831 |
| Metres to feet | 3.2808 | Cu metres to cu feet | 35.3147 |
| Yards to metres | 0.9144 | Cu yards to cu metres | 0.76455 |
| Metres to yards | 1.0936 | Cu metres to cu yards | 1.30795 |

| **Area** | | **Weight** | |
|---|---|---|---|
| Sq inches to sq centimetres | 6.4516 | Ounces to grams | 28.3495 |
| Sq centimetres to sq inches | 0.155 | Grams to ounces | 0.03527 |
| Sq feet to sq metres | 0.0929 | Pounds to grams | 453.59 |
| Sq metres to sq feet | 10.7639 | Grams to pounds | 0.002204 |
| Sq yards to sq metres | 0.8361 | Pounds to kilograms | 0.45359 |
| Sq metres to sq yards | 1.1959 | Kilograms to pounds | 2.2046 |

# Estimating and Costing

When estimating and costing for upholstery work, first break the job down into its constituent materials. The quantities required should be estimated, and the materials then costed from a current price catalogue. Amounts are totalled and 10% is added for sundries, such as twines, staples, tacks etc. The sundries figure may also include handling and the inevitable wastage of small materials.

The upholsterer normally adds an on-cost or mark-up to all materials used. This can vary a great deal and is calculated as a percentage of the wholesale cost of all the materials used in the workshop to produce upholstered work. The percentage added to materials may be as low as 25% or as high as 100%, often depending on the nature and the size of the business.

The following are worked examples of the process described above. The prices used are for exercise purposes only.

**1  Four traditional loose seats for dining chairs**

| | | | |
|---|---|---|---|
| a | Webbing 2in (51mm) black and white | 9ft 10in (3m) | £0.77 |
| b | Hessian 10oz 36in (91mm) | 39in (1m) | £0.25 |
| c | Curled hair | 4lbs | £7.72 |
| d | Calico 72in (183cm) | 39in (1m) | £2.65 |
| e | Skin wadding 32oz | 79in (2m) | £0.68 |
| f | Black bottom lining | 39in (1m) | £0.95 |
| g | Sundries (tacks, twine, staples etc) | 10% | £1.30 |
| h | On cost | 50% | £7.16 |
| | | Total | £21.48 |

**2   Two sprung, stuffover dining-chair seats**

| | | | |
|---|---|---|---|
| a | Webbing 2in (51mm) black and white | 23ft (7m) | £1.79 |
| b | Springs 5in (127mm) x 9½-gauge | 8 | £1.86 |
| c | Hessian 12oz 36in (91cm) | 19½in (½m) | £0.13 |
| d | Fibre for first stuffing | 4lbs | £3.16 |
| e | Scrim 72in (183cm) | 23½in (600m) | £0.81 |
| f | Curled hair | ½lb | £2.90 |
| g | Cotton felt 2½oz | 39in (1m) | £0.67 |
| h | Calico 72in (183cm) | 23½in (600mm) | £1.56 |
| i | Black lining cloth | 19½in (½m) | £0.50 |
| j | Sundries | 10% | £1.34 |
| k | On cost | 50% | £7.36 |
| | | Total | £22.08 |

**3   Twenty plywood seats for a set of boardroom chairs**

| | | | |
|---|---|---|---|
| a | Recon chipfoam 6lb x ⅞in (22mm) thick | 53.82 sq ft (5 sq m) | £32.00 |
| b | Foam CMHR 35 10mm (⅜in) thick | 53.82 sq ft (5 sq m) | £15.00 |
| c | Polyester wadding 4oz | 9ft 10in (3m) | £2.70 |
| d | Calico 72in (183cm) | 11ft 6in (3.5m) | £9.28 |
| e | Black lining 48in (122cm) | 16ft 5in (5m) | £2.50 |
| f | Sundries | 10% | £6.15 |
| g | On cost | 50% | £33.81 |
| | | Total | £101.44 |

# Estimating for covering materials

A cutting plan is essential for working out the amount of covering material that will be needed for a particular job. The cutting plan – even if it is a rough sketch – gives a clear picture of the piece parts to be cut within the limits of the cover type and its width. It also offers scope for adjustment and replanning to obtain the best cutting arrangement, allowing an economical use of materials.

A more accurate plan or layout becomes necessary when repetition of the work is likely. This can be used as a working drawing to be interpreted by others who may be involved in the work. An accurate plan is also advantageous when design and pattern are important so that matching and alignment of a cover design or motif is accurate and acceptable. A large or complex pattern on a cover can influence the amount of material that will eventually be required. Once the layout is drawn up and the amounts totalled, then changes can easily be made to the original, or an alternative and more advantageous plan can be produced.

Cover-cutting layouts are basically dimensioned drawings or sketches and they should give the following information:

● Length and width of material required
● Where joins will occur
● Visual display of all the parts
● Visual check on shapes and any waste areas
● A check on the essential pieces needed
● Use of extensions
● Use of fly pieces for economy

- Notching and centring, especially for sewn parts
- Amounts and lengths of piping strips needed
- Centring and alignment of design or pattern
- Exact shape of curves and facings

Chairs should preferably be measured for their cover either before they are stripped or at the calico stage. The vertical or length measurements taken from a chair are particularly important because it is these that, when added up, give the length of cover to be bought. Almost all chairs and settees have some left- and right-hand parts which are represented on the layout. One length measurement should give the amount needed for these parts, provided they fit within the cover width. If not, then each has to be placed separately along the cover length and the waste used up for some other small parts.

It is good practice to try to arrange for as many parts to pair as possible. This may sometimes mean using flies sewn to the sides of the inside back and to the inner ends of the inside arms etc. A cutting list is written out with measurements recorded at the widest and the longest points of each part. The length measurements are taken first followed by the widths, and the number of each part required.

| Job | | Cover | | Cutting plan |
|---|---|---|---|---|
| Cut parts | | Length | Width | |
| Inside back | IB | | | |
| Outside back | OB | | | |
| Inside arms | IA | | | |
| Outside arms | OA | | | |
| Seat | S | | | |
| Platform | PL | | | |
| Cushion | C | | | |
| Cushion borders | CB | | | |
| Inside wings | IW | | | |
| Outside wings | OW | | | |
| Arm facings | AF | | | |
| Back facings | BF | | | |
| Piping | P | | | |
| Others | | | | |

## Job estimate

The following is a typical job sheet for use when estimating for a job:

| Customer | Date | |
|---|---|---|
| Job | | Costing |
| **The Frame**<br>condition<br>repairs<br>restoration | estimate | £ |
| **The Cover**<br>type<br>design<br>width<br>length<br>repeat | | |
| | | £ |
| **Upholstery**<br>condition<br>replace<br>labour | materials<br><br>hours at £ | |
| trimmings | amounts | £ |
| | | £ |
| **Total** | | £ |
| Estimate:<br>Actual: | | |

# CHAPTER 10

# Information

## Fairs and Exhibitions

### January
Cologne International Furniture Fair, Cologne, Germany
Perspectives International Furniture Show, Paris, France

### February
The Furniture Show, NEC, Birmingham
SIT Exhibition - new chair design, at Business Design Centre, London
The Irish Furniture Show, Dublin, Eire

### March
CADCAM Exhibition, NEC, Birmingham
Practical Woodworker Show, Wembley Exhibition Centre, London

### April
High Point Furniture Market, High Point, North Carolina, USA
Milan International Furniture Fair, Milan, Italy
The Hanover Fair, Hanover, Germany

### May
Intahome Home Furnishing Show, Manchester G Mex, Manchester
Interzum Furniture Production Finishes and Furnishing Fair, Cologne, Germany
ICFF (International Contemporary Furniture Fair), New York, USA
IDI (Interior Design International), Olympia, London
BFM Classical Furniture Collection, Syon Park, London

### June/July
LIGNA International Wood Machinery Fair, Hanover, Germany
Degree shows in colleges throughout the UK
New designs (commercial and consumer) at Business Design Centre, London

### August
BFM Furniture Show, Manchester G Mex, Manchester

### September
Decosit International Upholstery Fabrics Fair, Brussels, Belgium
Decorex International Interior Design Show, Syon Park, London
Long Point, Guild of Furniture Manufacturers Show, Longeaton, Nottingham

### October/November
Techotel Contract Furniture and Furnishing Show, Genoa, Italy
Textiles Europe, Business Design Centre, London

# Glossary

**American cloth** An early form of leathercloth. Made from plain woven cotton coated on one side with linseed oil and other materials which make it waterproof.

**Antimacassar** Detachable cover for the backs of chairs and settees, originally used as a protection against Macassar hair oil.

**Armchair** Armed or arming chair as distinguished from a single or side chair having no arms.

**Back stool** An early single chair or side chair which developed from the stool and the chest. Later examples were upholstered.

**Ball fringe** A decorative trimming in which small balls, overwound with fine cord, hang at intervals among the long threads of the fringe.

**Balloon back chair** A name given to Victorian chairs with round or oval backs, mostly mahogany or rosewood, and upholstered seats.

**Bergéré** Louis XIV and XV style armchairs with upholstered backs and sides and squab-cushion seats. Later designs often have cane backs and sides.

**Binding** A narrow fabric used to support and finish an edge, such as a tape or a bias cut strip.

**Bolster arm** Large upholstered arm in a bolster shape – typical late nineteenth century.

**Bouclé** French name for a cloth with a rough-textured surface, produced by using a fancy yarn.

**Border** A long strip or wall of fabric used to form the sides or boxing on a cushion or mattress, for example.

**Box ottoman** A divan or couch with a hinged upholstered lid forming the seat, and storage space under.

**Braid** A flat, narrow woven fabric, used to decorate and finish upholstery, cushions and curtains.

**Bridling** A stitch used to hold down and stabilize scrim coverings, usually over first stuffings. A bridle stitch is a large running stitch, which penetrates and sets the depth of stuffing.

**Buckram** A material stiffened by the use of

45% weight of some agent such as size or glue.

**Bun foot** A turned, bun-shaped foot fitted to chairs and sofas – early 20th century.

**Calico** A white or unbleached cotton fabric with no printed design.

**Cambric** A fine, plain-weave cotton fabric, often glazed on one side, and used as a down-proof casing.

**Canapé** French name for a divan or sofa of Louis XV period or design.

**Cane edge** A sprung edge built on to a chair or bed using hourglass springs and a flexible cane.

**Canvas** A strong, heavyweight, plain-weave fabric, traditionally made from flax or cotton. Also a term often used by upholsterers to describe the first covering over webbings or springs.

**Casement** A plain-weave, even-textured, lightweight, all-cotton fabric. Traditionally used for sun curtains on south-facing windows.

**Chair bed** A low chair made from wood or metal which is dual function. The seat and back frames are completely adjustable for use as a single bed, with a minimum of three loose cushions.

**Chaise longue** French term for a couch or day bed with an upholstered back.

**Chenille** A pile fabric in which the weft thread is specially prepared and twisted by machinery, or woven and cut, before being woven into the yarn to form the pile. Cotton chenille is used in upholstery.

**Chill** The cast iron jointing block mounted on the head and foot ends of a metal bedstead. A chill, which may be single or double, has a tapered slot and supports the angle-iron bed frame.

**Chintz** A fine calico 35⁷⁄₁₆ or 47¼in (90 or 120cm) wide, usually roller or screen-printed and glazed or semi-glazed. Quilter chintz: Indian word meaning brightly coloured.

**Circ** A commonly used abbreviation for the small circular needles used for hand sewing and slip stitching of upholstery and soft furnishings.

**Collar** A strip of cover sewn into an inside back to provide a pull-in around an arm.

**Cosy corner** A seat with a high upholstered back which could be fitted into a corner and enable two or more people to sit together.

**Counterpane** A bed cover concealing bedding.

**Couch** A long upholstered seat with a back and one or two ends. Originally a double armchair.

**Cretonne** Originating from the French village of Creton and traditionally a copper-roller-printed cotton fabric. A term now more generally used to describe almost any type of lighter-weight floral printed cotton.

**Damask** Figured Jacquard fabric, the weft forming the design and the warp composed of a comparatively fine yarn making the background.

**Denier** The weight in grams of 9000 metres of filament yarn, e.g. silk.

**Divan chair** Fully upholstered armchair with long seat, often with scroll arms; late 19th century.

**Dogs** Large iron staples with sharpened ends. Used to brace and strengthen timber chair frames.

**Drop** A curtain measurement, taken from the fixing or hook level down to the hem. Headings and turnings are added to the drop.

**Duck** A strong, closely woven cloth of cotton or flax, similar to canvas. An average weight would be 10oz per square yard.

**Dug roll** Sometimes called a tack roll or thumb roll, it is formed around frame edges using small amounts of stuffing rolled up in hessian. Preformed dugging is produced from compressed paper or reconstituted chipfoam.

**Dyeing** Application of permanent colour to textile fibre, yarn or cloth.

**Easy chair** Originally the name given to winged upholstered armchairs, introduced about 1700, but now applies to upholstered armchairs generally.

**Embossing** A technique used on thick cloths and leathers to create relief patterns.

**Farthingale chair** An armless chair of the Stuart period, then used to accomodate ladies' hooped skirts.

**Feather down** The fine downy fibres cut and stripped from the quills of large feathers and used as a filling mixture.

**Feather edge** A fine top stitch applied to a stitched edge to create a sharp edge line.

**Fibre identification** Yarns taken from the warp and weft of a cloth and tested by burning, staining or microscopy to identify composition.

**Field bed** A canopy type of bed, easily dismantled.

**Filament** A very fine, long and usually continuous textile fibre. Several filaments of silk, for example, are spun together to produce one strong yarn.

**Flax** Strong, lustrous bast fibre taken from the stalk of the flax plant and woven into linen cloth.

**Fly piece** A narrow strip of fabric sewn to the edge of inside backs, inside arms or seats to economize on cover.

**Foldstool** A folding stool provided with a cushion for kneeling. Similar to a camp stool.

**French overlay** A soft, unsprung, unbordered mattress filled with layers of hair sandwiched between new wool.

**French work** The upholstery of chairs in the French style, using techniques such as diagonal stitching, feather edging, rope work and deep squab seats.

**Frise** An American term used to describe a moquette with cut or uncut pile woven from mohair.

**Futon** A simple Japanese floor bed or mattress made from strong cotton fabric and filled with cotton waste, tufted and unbordered. A futon is easily adapted and folded for sitting.

**Galoon** An old name for various kinds of braid used in upholstery.

**Garnett machine** Produces felted fillings, such as cotton and wool, in layered and cross-lapped form.

**Genoa velvet** A heavy velvet with a smooth ground weave and a pile figure in various colours.

**Gimp** Edgings as used in bedding and upholstery to decorate seams etc. Made from cotton, silk, rayons or mixtures.

**Hair cloth** An upholstery covering

material woven from the tail and mane hairs of horses, with cotton and rayons added. Plain and damask weaves are typical.

**Hessian (burlap)** A plain-woven cloth of flat yarns, usually jute, and made in 7 to 12oz weights.

**Hogrings** Small steel open-ended rings which are clinched to fix materials and pads to spring edges and units.

**India tape** Twill-woven 100% cotton tape similar to webbing and used to bind or reinforce edges.

**Kanaf** A natural textile fibre used as a substitute for jute and claimed to be rot-proof and very strong. Grown in the USA, Cuba and Russia.

**Knitting chair** An armless upholstered chair with a wooden drawer fitted under a seat.

**Knock down (KD) furniture** Pieces of furniture which may be easily folded, broken down or flat packed for distribution.

**Knock up** A mass-production system producing upholstered components for assembly and fitting before despatch.

**Laid cord** A very strong lashing cord in which the plies are laid together and not twisted.

**Line** The long, lustrous fibres stripped from the bast or stalk of the flax plant.

**Linters** Very fine cotton fibres taken from the seed after staple cotton has been removed.

**Lit** French name for a bed or mattress.

**Loose cover** A slip cover used over upholstered furniture. Traditionally employed in the summer season and made from cool linen union fabrics.

**Loose seat** Also called a slip seat, drop-in seat or pallet. An upholstered frame forming the seat of a dining chair supported on rebated rails.

**Love seat** The name given to a small seat on which two people can sit close together.

**Lug chair** Early English term for the wing type of easy chair.

**Mohair** The long fine hair of the Angora goat. Also describes an upholstery velvet made with a cotton base and a short mohair pile.

**Moiré** The fine-ribbed fabric with a 'watered' surface produced by heated pressure rollers, creating a reflective surface.

**Monks' cloth** For upholstery, a rough basket-weave fabric of cotton or jute.

**Monofilament** A fine continuous thread, usually synthetic. Transparent types are used as sewing threads.

**Moquette** Hard-wearing pile fabric, traditionally with a wool pile and cotton ground. Moquettes may be plain, figured, cut, uncut or frise.

**Morocco hide** Soft goat-skin leather, distinguished by its fine grain and texture. Much used by 18th-century upholsterers and cabinetmakers.

**Morris chair** Early 20th-century Arts-and-Crafts style chair with adjustable back, padded wooden arms and loose seat and back cushions.

**Motifs** The decorative figures in a pattern applied to or woven in a cloth.

**Nap** The surface of a fabric raised by combing or with abrasive rollers.

**Nursing chair** A 19th-century term for a single chair with a low seat 13–15in (325–375mm) high.

**Orris** Crimp used in upholstering laces of various designs in gold and silver.

**Ottoman** A long low seat without a back which originates from Turkey.

**Palliasse** A mattress stuffed with natural filling such as chaff or straw.

**Piece** An accepted unit length of fabric, ranging from 30 to 100m.

**Pile fabric** Fabric with a plain ground and an extra warp or weft, which projects to give the surface a fibrous nap.

**Pinstuffed** Shallow padded seat or back set into a rebated show-wood frame.

**Piping** Narrow strip of fabric folded and sewn into a seam. Used with or without a cord.

**Plain weave** A simple weave in which each warp thread interlaces over and under each weft thread. Also known as 'tabby weave'.

**Plush** A general term for pile fabrics which have a longer pile than velvet and are less closely woven.

**Pouffe** A stuffed footstool which stands high enough to be used as a seat.

**Presspahn** A strong, narrow strip of compressed cardboard used for back-tacking and reinforcing edges.

**Prie-dieu chair** A low-seated praying chair with a tall back and a narrow shelf.

**Pull-in upholstery (taped)** A fly or tape sewn into a covered surface and pulled in to create a waisted effect. May also be hand stitched through the cover surface.

**Ramie** China grass, providing a strong, lustrous fibre resembling silk.

**Repp** A heavy and firmly woven wool fabric with

transverse ribs; used for upholstery.

**Rollover arm**   A style of easy-chair arm upholstery with a strong, rollover scroll shape.

**Ruching**   Narrow, knitted decorative trimming with a heading and a cut or looped surface. Used generally in place of piping around cushions and edges.

**Scrim**   Plain, open-weave cloth with hard twisted yarns, woven from jute, cotton or flax. Used in upholstery to cover first stuffings.

**Scrollover arm**   An arm which curves inwards from the seat of a chair in the form of a double scroll, breaking into a convex sweep before curving back to form an arm rest.

**Seating**   Upholsterers' term for hard-wearing cloths, for example hair cloth.

**Settee**   A name derived from the 17th-century settle. It is usually made from wood with a high back, large enough for several people.

**Shadow fabric**   A cloth in which the warp yarn is printed prior to the cloth being woven.

**Skiving**   A technique used to trim leather with a knife to a fine feather edge and produce a scarf joint. Thin skivers of leather are used to trim surfaces in cabinet work.

**Slip cover**   Alternative name given to a loose or detachable cover.

**Smoker's chair**   A club easy chair, covered in leather, with a 'D' or tub shape.

**Sofa**   This term first appeared in the late 17th century and described a couch for reclining.

**Spinneret**   The stainless steel nozzle drilled with fine holes through which synthetic fibre filaments are formed by extrusion, e.g. Rayon, Nylon, Terylene.

**Spoon back**   The shape of a chair back, Queen Anne style, curved to fit the shape of the body.

**Squab**   A loose cushion.

**Stitch up**   A stuffed and shaped edge, reinforced with rows of blind and top stitches.

**Stuffover**   The name given to a chair or settee frame which is almost entirely covered with upholstery.

**Tapestry**   The original term applies to a wool fabric woven by hand, and later to power-woven imitations, figured upholstery fabrics, and to fabric where designs are partly or wholly formed by the warp.

**Tester**   A canopy built or suspended above a bed as a frame or rails to support curtains.

**Trimming**   The applying or forming of decorative effects using fabrics.

**Tub chair**   A large easy chair with a concave back.

**Tufting**   The technique of bridling and compressing stuffed areas in chairs, cushions and mattresses to hold fillings in place and set a depth and firmness of feel.

**Turkey work**   Hand-knotting of wool into canvas to produce fabrics and carpets.

**Upholstery**   Fabric furnishings, or upholstery as we know it, began as a craft in chair making and bed making at the end of the 16th century.

**Valance**   A length of fabric which may be pleated or gathered and used to conceal a rail or frame. Generally associated with bedding.

**Vandyke**   The term used in upholstery to describe a type of sewn joint in deep buttoning work. Traditionally, a hand-stitched joint used in fine leather work and carefully hidden in the pleating between buttons.

**Velour**   A fine cotton velvet originating in France.

**Velveteen**   A very fine, lightweight cotton pile fabric with a weft pile; not of upholstery weight.

**Warp**   A yarn which runs in the length direction of a cloth.

**Weft**   A yarn which forms the cross threads in a cloth, selvedge to selvedge.

**Welt**   To conceal or decorate a fabric or leather joint. It also increases strength.

**Worsted**   Made from long wool yarn fibres, combed and twisted hard.

**X-frame chair**   Early 17th-century chair, upholstered and decorated with nails and fringe. Became popular during the reign of James I e.g. the Winchester chair.

# Index

# About the Author

David James was born in High Wycombe, and has worked in upholstery since leaving school. After a number of years as an instructor in a factory, he joined the Ministry of Public Buildings and Works as a technical officer, gaining a National Furnishing Diploma. In 1966 he became a lecturer in upholstery at Buckinghamshire College of Higher Education, near his home in Marlow, and was promoted to senior lecturer in 1971.

He is an honorary member of the City and Guilds of London Institute, and has been awarded their licentiateship. He is also a member of the Guild of Traditional Upholsterers. In recent years he has turned his talents to writing and illustrating. He has written two books: *Upholstery: A Complete Course* (1990), and *Upholstery Techniques and Projects* (1994). He has also made two videos: *The Traditional Upholstery Workshop, Part 1: Drop-in and Pinstuffed Seats*, and *The Traditional Upholstery Workshop, Part 2: Stuffover Upholstery* (both 1994).

# TITLES AVAILABLE FROM
# GMC Publications

## BOOKS

### WOODWORKING

| | |
|---|---|
| 40 More Woodworking Plans & Projects | GMC Publications |
| Bird Boxes and Feeders for the Garden | Dave Mackenzie |
| Complete Woodfinishing | Ian Hosker |
| David Charlesworth's Furniture-making Techniques | |
| | David Charlesworth |
| Electric Woodwork | Jeremy Broun |
| Furniture & Cabinetmaking Projects | GMC Publications |
| Furniture Projects | Rod Wales |
| Furniture Restoration (Practical Crafts) | Kevin Jan Bonner |
| Furniture Restoration and Repair for Beginners | |
| | Kevin Jan Bonner |
| Furniture Restoration Workshop | Kevin Jan Bonner |
| Green Woodwork | Mike Abbott |
| Making & Modifying Woodworking Tools | Jim Kingshott |
| Making Chairs and Tables | GMC Publications |
| Making Fine Furniture | Tom Darby |
| Making Little Boxes from Wood | John Bennett |
| Making Shaker Furniture | Barry Jackson |
| Making Woodwork Aids and Devices | Robert Wearing |

| | |
|---|---|
| Pine Furniture Projects for the Home | Dave Mackenzie |
| Router Magic: Jigs, Fixtures and Tricks to | |
| Unleash your Router's Full Potential | Bill Hylton |
| Routing for Beginners | Anthony Bailey |
| The Scrollsaw: Twenty Projects | John Everett |
| Sharpening Pocket Reference Book | Jim Kingshott |
| Sharpening: The Complete Guide | Jim Kingshott |
| Space-Saving Furniture Projects | Dave Mackenzie |
| Stickmaking: A Complete Course | Andrew Jones & Clive George |
| Stickmaking Handbook | Andrew Jones & Clive George |
| Test Reports: The Router and | |
| Furniture & Cabinetmaking | GMC Publications |
| Veneering: A Complete Course | Ian Hosker |
| Woodfinishing Handbook (Practical Crafts) | Ian Hosker |
| Woodworking Plans and Projects | GMC Publications |
| Woodworking with the Router: Professional | |
| Router Techniques any Woodworker can Use | Bill Hylton & Fred Matlack |
| The Workshop | Jim Kingshott |

### WOODTURNING

| | |
|---|---|
| Adventures in Woodturning | David Springett |
| Bert Marsh: Woodturner | Bert Marsh |
| Bill Jones' Notes from the Turning Shop | Bill Jones |
| Bill Jones' Further Notes from the Turning Shop | Bill Jones |
| Colouring Techniques for Woodturners | Jan Sanders |
| The Craftsman Woodturner | Peter Child |
| Decorative Techniques for Woodturners | Hilary Bowen |
| Essential Tips for Woodturners | GMC Publications |
| Faceplate Turning | GMC Publications |
| Fun at the Lathe | R.C. Bell |
| Illustrated Woodturning Techniques | John Hunnex |
| Intermediate Woodturning Projects | GMC Publications |
| Keith Rowley's Woodturning Projects | Keith Rowley |
| Make Money from Woodturning | Ann & Bob Phillips |
| Multi-Centre Woodturning | Ray Hopper |
| Pleasure and Profit from Woodturning | Reg Sherwin |
| Practical Tips for Turners & Carvers | GMC Publications |

| | |
|---|---|
| Practical Tips for Woodturners | GMC Publications |
| Spindle Turning | GMC Publications |
| Turning Miniatures in Wood | John Sainsbury |
| Turning Wooden Toys | Terry Lawrence |
| Understanding Woodturning | Ann & Bob Phillips |
| Useful Techniques for Woodturners | GMC Publications |
| Useful Woodturning Projects | GMC Publications |
| Woodturning: Bowls, Platters, Hollow Forms, Vases, | |
| Vessels, Bottles, Flasks, Tankards, Plates | GMC Publications |
| Woodturning: A Foundation Course | Keith Rowley |
| Woodturning: A Source Book of Shapes | John Hunnex |
| Woodturning Jewellery | Hilary Bowen |
| Woodturning Masterclass | Tony Boase |
| Woodturning Techniques | GMC Publications |
| Woodturning Tools & Equipment Test Reports | |
| | GMCPublications |
| Woodturning Wizardry | David Springet |

### WOODCARVING

| | |
|---|---|
| The Art of the Woodcarver | GMC Publications |
| Carving Birds & Beasts | GMC Publications |
| Carving on Turning | Chris Pye |
| Carving Realistic Birds | David Tippey |
| Decorative Woodcarving | Jeremy Williams |
| Essential Tips for Woodcarvers | GMC Publications |
| Essential Woodcarving Techniques | Dick Onians |
| Lettercarving in Wood: A Practical Course | Chris Pye |
| Power Tools for Woodcarving | David Tippey |
| Practical Tips for Turners & Carvers | GMC Publications |
| Relief Carving in Wood: A Practical Introduction | Chris Pye |

| | |
|---|---|
| Understanding Woodcarving | GMC Publications |
| Understanding Woodcarving in the Round | GMC Publications |
| Useful Techniques for Woodcarvers | GMC Publications |
| Wildfowl Carving - Volume 1 | Jim Pearce |
| Wildfowl Carving - Volume 2 | Jim Pearce |
| The Woodcarvers | GMC Publications |
| Woodcarving: A Complete Course | Ron Butterfield |
| Woodcarving: A Foundation Course | Zoë Gertner |
| Woodcarving for Beginners | GMC Publications |
| Woodcarving Tools & Equipment Test Reports | GMC Publications |
| Woodcarving Tools, Materials & Equipment | Chris Pye |

### UPHOLSTERY

| | |
|---|---|
| Seat Weaving (Practical Crafts) | Ricky Holdstock |
| Upholsterer's Pocket Reference Book | David James |
| Upholstery: A Complete Course | David James |

| | |
|---|---|
| Upholstery Restoration | David James |
| Upholstery Techniques & Projects | David James |